Mindful Prayer

A Clinical Approach to Achieving a Deeper Spiritual Connection

NORMAN GOLDWASSER, Ph.D.

Published by
Horizon Psychological Services
MIAMI BEACH, FLORIDA

ISBN: Softcover: 979-8-9938293-0-2
        Hardcover: 979-8-9938293-1-9

Cover and Interior: Gary A. Rosenberg • www.thebookcouple.com
Editing: Erica Meyer Rauzin

Printed in the United States of America

Contents

Introduction: My Reasons for Writing This Book.......1

1. What Is Prayer? 5

2. Mindfulness 15

3. Applying Mindfulness to Prayer....................... 29

4. Intentionality.. 43

5. Impediments to Mindful Prayer........................51

6. Solutions to Overcoming Impediments............... 77

7. Maintenance...103

Conclusion: The Rewards of Achieving a Deeper
    Connection.. 111

Acknowledgments 115

About the Author.. 117

The world has become a complicated, even frightening place for many of us—with wars, protests, hate, and confusion intruding into our daily lives. If ever there was a time that we needed to deepen our spiritual connection, this is the time. But, yet, finding our way to be better connected spiritually and to pray mindfully has become that much more challenging. If ever there was a time for meaningful prayer, this is it.

This book is as much a part of my spiritual journey as it is an effort to assist others in theirs. In my daily life, I am surrounded by people who have managed to connect with God or their higher power in ways that are truly awe-inspiring. I dedicate this book to them and to all those who are still struggling to achieve that higher level of connection…which may include you, since you chose to read it.

My Reasons for Writing This Book

As an Orthodox Jew, my faith centers around prayer as a daily cornerstone of my spirituality. Prayer is established as an ongoing relationship with God and a means by which I can feel connected to Him on a regular basis. The daily ritual of prayer is designed to maintain that connection over the long run and to preserve our commitment to our faith. Prayer is also an opportunity to set aside the concerns and troubles of the day and transcend to a different level of being, one that allows us to clear our minds and have a deeper soul-level experience.

Over 35 years of practice as a clinical psychologist, however, I have experienced countless numbers of patients of all faiths who have shared their personal struggles with prayer, explaining how difficult it is to be able to pray in a focused and "real" way. They struggled with the ability to establish a genuine spiritual connection. Indeed, they found that a variety of factors impeded their ability to pray mindfully and left them feeling frustrated and empty. They wanted to connect through prayer, but did not have the ability. So, they either went through the motions, stopped going to prayer services, stopped trying to pray, or disconnected from religious obser-vance altogether.

Many of these patients slipped into depression because they considered this a failure, or they felt disconnected from their roots. Others found various other ways to have a spiritual experience, but still felt that their inability to pray effectively left a void inside of them. They still yearned to communicate with God through the language of prayer, whether it was formulaic and formal, or organic and personal.

The purpose of this book is to examine the various rea-sons why people find meaningful prayer challenging, and to explore what you can do to enhance your prayer experience, whatever your faith is. Many books have been written about prayer, with the goal of enhancing our connection to prayer. This book is different. It's a unique look at the issues that impede mindful prayer from a more clinical perspective and an examination of various types of psychological and per-sonality issues that could interfere with the ability to pray mindfully. Perhaps more importantly, it offers real solutions to the challenges people face when they try to pray mindfully.

A Personal Perspective

On a more personal note, the idea for this book came not only from my experiences with patients who struggle with their ability to pray in a focused, mindful way, but also from my own experiences. Although I would not necessarily diag-nose myself as being clinically obsessive or having OCD, I do find my mind wandering from my morning prayers as I think about my upcoming schedule, patients I will be seeing, or personal challenges that I have faced or will soon face. Similarly, at night, events that I experienced during the day crop up in my mind while I am engaged in prayer and, before I know it, I am completely distracted and derailed from the prayer experience.

I find this extremely frustrating, and too often I have to redirect my attention, or just start over and try to focus on the actual prayers, concentrating on what is in my heart instead of what is in my head. Sometimes I actually succeed and get back on track, but sadly, other times I am just too distracted by pressing concerns to reset my mind toward praying mindfully.

So, writing this book is actually as much of a personal journey to reconnect more deeply to my Maker as it is an attempt to enable others to have a more successful experience of connecting with God through prayer. I hope that through reading this book, both you and I can reach a higher level of focused, mindful prayer that can leave us with a greatly enhanced ability to feel spiritually connected, emotionally fulfilled, and personally grounded.

Structure of the Book

After this introductory chapter, the book begins in Chapter 1 by focusing on how we can define prayer and the various reasons why we pray, or why we should pray, in the first place.

Chapter 2 focuses on the concept of mindfulness in more general terms, including its definitions and origins, and what it actually means to be mindful.

In Chapter 3, the book takes a deeper look into the concept of mindfulness. It focuses on how we can apply mindfulness to the experience of prayer in ways that can help make it more meaningful and can help us achieve a deeper spiritual connection.

Chapter 4 focuses on the key concept of intentionality, exploring how intentions can help us orient ourselves toward effective prayer.

In Chapter 5, the book pivots to the topic of impediments that can interfere with our ability to pray mindfully. This is a more clinical approach to the topic, since it discusses various conditions and disorders that make focused prayer difficult.

Chapter 6 discusses specific solutions that can help those who wish to pray mindfully to overcome these impediments.

Chapter 7 deals with the all-important goal of maintaining a mindful prayer practice. It explains how to ensure that the gains you achieve by using this book's methods endure over time.

Finally, the book concludes with an important and encouraging overview of the various rewards you can experience by achieving the goal of mindful prayer. I hope you will feel inspired to try to implement these strategies in order to achieve the overarching goal of attaining a greater spiritual connection and, ultimately, becoming a better version of yourself.

You will also find case histories and personal testimonials from people who used this approach to achieve more mindful prayer. They share how it enhanced their lives at a spiritual level and increased their general sense of personal well-being.

CHAPTER 1

What Is Prayer?

Connecting

Prayer means different things to different people. For most, however, its primary goal is to connect with God, or some form of a Higher Power. For theists—those who believe in the existence of a God who is alive and who has an active role in our lives—connecting is an important part of life, whether several times a day, daily, or weekly. The experience of connecting with our Creator can be an important, if not essential, part of daily life. It can give us a sense of security that we are not alone and that we have a Higher Being who is there for us. We can have faith that God runs the world and has a direct impact on us, at a personal, familial, communal, and global level.

For many who are isolated or alienated from family, or who have lost important relationships through illness, death, divorce, or disability, being able to connect to a Higher Power can fill the void that is left when personal relationships are lost. If you are alone, you can find comfort in knowing that you always have God in your life and that you can use personal prayer to connect with Him at any time.

For those whose religious observance includes daily communal prayer, such as Mass in Catholicism, Salah prayers in Islam, or Minyanim in Judaism, you also experience connections by being with other people who have gathered for prayers. The shared experience of coming together for communal prayer can provide a meaningful sense of belonging, especially for those who otherwise feel that they don't belong anywhere else in their lives. This common connection can make an enormous difference for people who are isolated and alone.

Others have found that prayer can actually help facilitate a sense of internal connection within themselves. Taking time out of your busy schedule to pray can help you introspect and connect with what is going on in your mind, heart, and soul. We often lose that intrapersonal connection to ourselves when we are preoccupied with the stresses of parenting, job responsibilities, interpersonal conflicts, addictive behaviors, and other distractions that keep us from looking inward. Having a structured prayer routine can help you find the time to get off the hamster wheel of life, take a break, reconnect with yourself, and get in touch with what you are feeling or needing, or whatever is causing you pain. It can also keep you from losing yourself and help you maintain the steady dose of self-reflection and self-awareness that we all need to achieve for healthy emotional equilibrium.

Finding meaning

Many of us find ourselves caught up in the fast pace of daily life, struggling to keep up with the expectations we have of ourselves, or that we feel others have for us, whether that entails financial or vocational achievement, appearance, status, or popularity. The explosion of social media has exponentially amplified the need to be "liked" and has intensified the fear of missing out (FOMO) that pervades our lives as social beings in the modern world.

Wherever I travel, and wherever I go for local appointments or evenings out, people are glued to their phones, scrolling through their Instagram feeds, or following the latest "influencer" who is giving advice about how to advance in one way or another. Any sense of meaning gets lost in this confluence of social pressure and the need to "get ahead." What is this life about anyway? What is the end goal of your life? How can you find meaning in your life, and how do you define what is actually meaningful?

For many of us, prayer can add meaning to our lives through the connections it provides. Having a meaningful connection with God and with those who join with you to pray can give your life a greater sense of purpose. It can help you transcend the superficial and the mundane and embrace a deeper, more meaningful experience in your daily life. Prayer can also help you put things in perspective and focus on what is truly meaningful.

Asking for help

We all face challenges, and the feeling that we have to deal with them on our own can be daunting and lonely. Knowing that a Higher Power is actively involved in world events at a macro level and also shapes our day-to-day lives at a more micro level can be empowering. It can provide much-needed hope and reassurance that things will turn out OK in the end. This concept of divine providence, the idea that God takes care of us and has a direct effect on what happens to us, underlies the view that prayer is a way for us to reach out for God's assistance, asking for help in achieving whatever we need.

This can apply when we are distressed and desperate for help, or on an ongoing basis, even if we are not particularly distressed at the time. Praying for health, sustenance, and overall well-being for ourselves and our loved ones can be deeply satisfying, especially if we believe that it can actually help achieve a positive outcome. Knowing that a Higher Power has your back and can help you in very real terms with your struggles can be extremely reassuring and empowering.

Focusing on others

Praying for the welfare of others—those in our lives and those who are not, but who we know are suffering and need help—can be extremely powerful, both for the person who is praying and the recipients of those prayers.

Judaism has a tradition of praying for the sick, knowing that it can be of enormous help in facilitating healing. A well-known and remarkable study found that those in precarious medical conditions for whom others prayed actively on a regular basis fared significantly better medically than those for whom prayer was not instituted. In an even more remarkable finding, the study reported that neither group of patients knew whether people were praying for them or not. Yet, the impact of the prayers was significant and unmistakable.

This effect of prayer on the well-being of others is a dramatic example of the power of prayer to influence events in our lives. The fact that the study found statistically significant outcomes beyond what could be expected by chance clearly indicates that prayer can achieve profound results. But its impact goes beyond the outcome. Praying for others can also have a profound impact on those who are praying.

In today's "me" world, which reinforces a narcissistic emphasis on ourselves and our appearance, accomplishments, financial success, and status reports on social media, taking the time to pray for others who need our prayers can be a significant antidote to society's pervasive cultural narcissism. It can allow us to develop and build empathy within ourselves and make us better people.

A Personal Note

When I was much younger and working as an intern at the Veterans Administration hospital in Richmond, Virginia, I unfortunately became paralyzed after getting a flu shot that I was required to have because one of my rotations was in the hospital's heart transplant unit. Patients there receive an immunosuppressant drug called cyclosporine, which helps to prevent their bodies from rejecting their new heart. All staff members working on the unit were required to get a flu shot because our patients were immunologically compromised and, therefore, very vulnerable if they became infected with influenza.

Two weeks after I received the shot, I started to experience strange sensations in my arms and lower extremities, including severe weakness. I eventually lost my ability to move altogether. I was diagnosed with a rare autoimmune disorder called Guillain-Barré Syndrome (GBS) and was intubated on a respirator. I was in the Intensive Care Unit for six weeks and then hospitalized for three months.

My unusual saga became known throughout the Jewish community, both in America and abroad. Letters (this was pre-internet, so email didn't exist) and phone calls poured in asking for my Hebrew name, which is necessary in reciting the special Jewish prayer for healing the sick.

Years later, I would run into people who told me they were still praying for my recovery. Words alone cannot describe the gratitude, support, and love I felt toward the people who cheered me on through prayer.

However, I'll never forget what one old friend from Florida, Meira Davis, who had also moved there from Richmond, told me years after my hospitalization. It stood out for its impact and profundity. When she told me that she was still praying for me after all those years, I became emotional and profusely thanked her for keeping me in her prayers. She responded, "You don't understand. I've known you since you were a kid, and I have been doing this as much for me as for you. Knowing what you were going through and that there was nothing I could do to help was extremely upsetting for me. Being able to pray every day for your recovery gave me a sense of purpose and allowed me to feel less helpless, knowing that at least I could pray for you."

Amazing

While I was in rehabilitation, the doctors and therapists cautioned me about having unrealistic expectations about my ultimate recovery. They told me that a significant percentage of GBS patients never recover fully, and many end up in wheelchairs or braces for the rest of their lives. They also told me that I should expect that the remyelination of my nerves (the recovery of nerve functioning) would continue for, at the most, two or three years. However, I experienced a continuing improvement of functioning that lasted over decades, to the extent that I now have only minor deficits in certain muscle groups and less stamina than I had before the onset of GBS. Otherwise, my recovery has been, thank God, almost complete and sustained. I can't help but believe that all of the praying on my behalf had a tremendous impact on my recovery, to the extent that I exceeded every medical expectation.

Such is the power of prayer.

Getting Clarity

When life gets rough and the world becomes too much, it's easy to become confused and overwhelmed. Our limbic system, the emotional center of the brain, can get overactivated and interfere with our ability to process our experiences.

The amygdala is the almond-shaped core of the brain's limbic system, where we feel emotions most intensely. The terms "limbic hijack" or "amygdala hijack" describe what happens when we get so emotionally overloaded that we get derailed, and it becomes difficult to think clearly and work things through. In this state of mind, we are not capable of putting things in perspective and looking at the larger picture. Our emotions take over, and we cannot see beyond them.

Engaging in prayer can allow us to shift out of the limbic system and engage the brain's processing centers, enabling us to get beyond the intensity of our emotions. Then, we are able to see the big picture—that God runs the world and we don't, and that allowing ourselves to get over-stressed only inhibits our ability to process our worries and cope more effectively with our challenges.

Achieving Serenity

Think of serenity as akin to peace of mind or a deep sense of calm. Many of us live our lives with a great deal of unease and uncertainty, be it in regard to our personal lives or more global issues such as devastating wars, political instability, the rise of anti-Semitism and anti-Western values, and violent protests throughout the world. It has become increasingly more difficult to achieve a sense of inner peace with the swirling maelstrom of turmoil that permeates our lives.

Prayer can often be effective in allowing us to disconnect from the madness we are witnessing and reminding us that

God runs the world, not us, and that He is ultimately in charge. Prayer can assist us in reorienting to that reality, which helps us achieve a deeper level of serenity, knowing that the chaos will work out in the end, according to God's plan.

Borrowing from the 12-step world, I have found the *Serenity Prayer* to be an immensely useful tool for helping me focus on how I can achieve serenity when dealing with difficult situations or stressful people in my practice or personal life. It helps me redirect from the false expectation of being able to control events or other people. It also enables me to gain the proper perspective, which leads to a more serene place inside my mind and calms the physical reactions in my body.

EXERCISE 1: SERENITY PRAYER

When you face a difficult challenge and wish to engage in prayer to reach a state of serenity that helps you cope, repeat this phrase to yourself several times, or until you feel that you are ready to start praying from a place of serenity, rather than from one of stress or consternation:

> *"God, grant me the strength to change what I can, the courage to accept what I cannot change, and the wisdom to know the difference."*

CHAPTER 2

Mindfulness

Definitions

According to the *New Oxford American Dictionary,* mindfulness means "the quality or state of being conscious or aware of something," or more to the point of this discussion, "a mental state achieved by focusing one's awareness on the present moment, while calmly acknowledging and accepting one's feeling, thoughts, and bodily sensations." Many different aspects of mindfulness have emerged over the years, including:

➤ Non-judging   ➤ Acceptance

➤ Gratitude   ➤ Generosity

➤ Patience   ➤ Connecting

➤ Trust   ➤ Letting go

As you can see, these attributes of mindfulness can be enormously useful in helping us prepare for, connect with, and envelop ourselves in prayer. Disconnecting from negative judgments about other people can open our hearts to connect with our Creator and focus on gratitude for all that He has given us. Being mindful can allow us to be more patient amidst the flurry of competing thoughts, time pressures, and demands. This can help us focus instead on connecting with God through prayer.

Trusting in God and knowing that He runs the world, loves us and wants what is ultimately best for us, even if we are struggling with the challenges we face, can facilitate a deeper connection to Him when we are engaged in prayer. Radical acceptance of these challenges, with the knowledge that they are all for our ultimate good and that they promote our growth and development, can assist us in giving ourselves over to God, and allow us to be more engaged in prayer.

Praying for others in need, for our community, or for the increasingly complex and dangerous world we are living in can help us shift our focus away from our own challenges. This other-focused orientation can also promote our generosity of spirit. As previously mentioned, prayer can also allow us to connect to others, to God, and to our authentic selves. Those who pray tend to be more connected people, in general. Finally, mindfulness allows us to focus entirely on the present moment, instead of dwelling on what happened in the past or worrying about the future. This can help us "let go…and let God." It can also help us envelop ourselves in the emotional and spiritual connection that we can experience when we are fully engaged in prayer.

Origins

Mindfulness originally evolved from the Buddhist practice of meditation, which was developed more than 2,600 years ago. It grew out of the concept of *"sati,"* which is loosely translated as moment-to-moment awareness. Meditation was seen as a contemplative state based on the Four Foundations, being mindful of body, feelings, mind, and *"dhammas,"* or phenomena. It was seen as a "liberation from suffering" and a means by which we can separate ourselves from feelings of distress and hopelessness.

Although the practice of mindfulness originates primarily from the Buddhist tradition of meditation, the concept can be found in all major religious traditions. In Judaism, *"hitbodedut,"* which comes from the Breslov sect of Hasidism, is an intense self-seclusion that promotes a deep, personal meditative experience in which we can communicate our deepest thoughts, feelings, and requests to God. In Christianity, mysticism was the wellspring behind the movement toward meditation, which allowed people of faith to move away from structured prayer and toward a more spontaneous spiritual experience of communicating with God at a more personal and emotional level. In Islam, the concept of *"murqabah"* means "to watch, observe, or regard something attentively." It enables believers to divest themselves completely from their daily lives and focus on the awareness of Allah's presence.

The practice of mindfulness has permeated the thinking and lifestyle of all major religions as a conceptual conduit to a deeper spiritual connection. It hopefully allows us to enter into a state of being where we can establish an in-the-moment awareness of the present, open our hearts and souls, and commune with God on a deeper, more personal level.

Achieving Mindfulness

Anchoring the Mind

Our minds are at once wonderful, complex, and often perplexing. We often think about a myriad of different things, dwelling on events that happened in the past, planning for or worrying about outcomes in the future, or thinking about everything on our plates that needs our attention. We often jump from one focus to another in a peripatetic stream of consciousness that can leave us feeling "all over the place."

With a mind like that, it is no wonder that focusing on mindful prayer can be a daunting task, to say the least. But there are strategies you can use to succeed.

For instance, anchoring is a well-established method within the world of mindfulness. It helps us harness our minds' intense and ever-changing shifts of attention and maintain a singular focus by anchoring our minds through our senses. You can achieve this visually by focusing intently on a particular object, tactilely through the sense of touch by holding something soft or textured, olfactorily through the smell of something real or imagined, or cognitively through a mantra that prevents you from being distracted and unfocused.

You can achieve anchoring by deciding—either *a priori* or in the moment—how you wish to ground your mind, and then singularly focusing on the chosen object, touch, smell, or mantra, excluding everything else. This is a wonderful way to still the mind and prepare ourselves to enter a state of being that will allow us to engage in more mindful prayer. It is a way to calm the frenetic pace of our thoughts so we can exclusively focus on what is most important in the moment, connecting with God through meaningful, uplifting prayer.

To achieve mindfulness through the practice of anchoring, think freestyle; focus on the thoughts in your mind. Then begin using your chosen anchor, focusing exclusively on that technique, be it seeing, hearing, smelling, or touching. Observe how your mind lets go of all competing thoughts, ruminations, and obsessions. Focus only on the anchor that you have chosen. You will be amazed at the power you have to rein in your overactive mind and focus on what truly matters to you—in this case, praying in a more mindful and focused manner.

EXERCISE 2: ANCHORING

Before engaging in prayer, try this anchoring technique to help narrow your focus on a singular object and release competing thoughts:

Choose an object in the room where you are now, and then focus on that object to the exclusion of everything else. Allow your focus to rest only on that object, and divert your mind from focusing on anything else that may compete for your attention. Stay focused on that object for several minutes or until you feel that you have managed to block out competing thoughts and stopped focusing on anything else in the room.

Then, gently transition to the beginning of the prayer you wish to concentrate on. As you engage, focus on the prayer to the exclusion of everything else. Stay focused on that prayer until you complete it. Be aware of your thoughts. If your mind begins to wander, redirect it back to the prayer, keeping in mind the anchoring technique you used before starting to pray.

Breathing

Deep breathing is another way to achieve mindfulness and to focus away from stressful thoughts and anxious feelings. Our pulmonary system is the only system in our bodies over which we can maintain voluntary control. We obviously can't control our heart rate, endocrine system, galvanic skin response, or any other organ in our body. However, through controlled, intentional breathing techniques, we can have a direct impact on our nervous system and, thereby, have some degree of control over stress, anxiety, or other negative emotions that impact our ability to be mindful.

We all have a fight-or-flight response that emanates from the sympathetic nervous system. It reacts to real (or perceived) threats by releasing stress hormones such as cortisol, adrenaline, and noradrenaline. These hormones activate the organ systems in the body that are necessary for us to react when we are threatened. Many people with stressful lives find that their sympathetic nervous system becomes overactive. This creates a state of mind that makes it difficult, if not impossible, to be calm enough to be mindful. Therefore, we must control the sympathetic nervous system in order to prepare ourselves for prayer that is truly mindful.

So, how do we do that? The sympathetic nervous system has a competitor: the parasympathetic nervous system, which runs parallel to the nerves of the sympathetic nervous system (para is the Latin word for "next to"). Unlike the sympathetic nervous system, which activates the fight-or-flight response, the parasympathetic nervous system promotes relaxation and calms the overall nervous system. These two systems are mutually exclusive; when one is activated, the other shuts down, and vice versa. Our goal is to activate the parasympathetic nervous system and ultimately enable the body, and, hopefully, the mind, to relax and allow mindfulness to set in.

Deep breathing is the best way to do this because it directly activates the parasympathetic nervous system. Countless breathing strategies have been developed over the years, with varying elements, sequences, and time parameters. I have found that most, if not all, of these strategies are overly complicated and time-consuming. People who are stressed or anxious typically don't have the patience or time to go through a prolonged breathing routine, so I developed one that is simple and rather quick:

EXERCISE 3: CDRC

CDRC is the acronym that I came up with to describe the four steps of this breathing routine. It's actually only three steps, but the last step repeats the first:

- **C**leansing breath
- **R**hythmic breathing
- **D**eep breathing
- **C**leansing breath

It works like this:

Find a comfortable place to sit or lie down, and close your eyes.

- **C**leansing Breath—This is co-opted from Lamaze, the early natural childbirth method. Begin with a deep, slow, inhaled breath, count to three, and then exhale a forceful, protracted breath until your lungs are completely empty. Count to three again before repeating this sequence. Do it only twice, because doing it repeatedly can lead to hyperventilation. The cleansing breath is a method of clearing sur-face-level tension and stress from the body and the nervous system and becoming more open to deeper levels of relaxation.

- **D**eep Breathing—This step begins with taking the same deep, slow inhaled breath and counting to three. This time, instead of a forceful exhale, slowly let go of your breath in a more relaxed, gentle man-ner, taking as long as possible. Count again to three before inhaling again, and repeat the sequence three to five times until you achieve a deeper sense of calm.

- **R**hythmic Breathing—This is a more regular rhythm of breathing that follows a relaxed "in...and out, in... and out" pattern. It resembles the pattern of normal breathing, but it is slower and more calming. Do this for three to five minutes. Visualize a calming scene, like a sunset over the water, a pastoral landscape, or a lazy river.

- **C**leansing Breath—Take one more cleansing breath to close out the exercise.

Notice how much calmer you feel, and how much clearer your mind is. Feel the reduced tension in your body and your improved ability to enter a mental state of mindfulness and to engage in a deeper prayer experience.

Meditation

As previously discussed, the ancient Buddhist practice of meditation has been adapted more recently by various faiths. It has also been developed as a psychological technique to help people become more present in the moment, and achieve a deeper sense of calm.

A variety of methods and apps can help you develop a meditation practice, and I encourage you to explore these various options online.

However, I am presenting you with a simple meditation technique that can more easily transport you to a deeper state of calm and enable you to feel the sense of presence and awareness that can lead to mindfulness:

EXERCISE 4: SPIRITUAL MEDITATION

Introduction

This meditation can help you prepare for a mindful prayer experience. Once you are familiar with the meditation process, you will be able to meditate on your own, unguided. There is no right or wrong way to meditate. The most important thing you can do is adopt a passive attitude—allowing, not forcing. Experiencing, not controlling. Don't worry about meditating the "right" way—just let it happen however it happens without worrying about the outcome.

It is normal to have many extraneous thoughts going through your mind while meditating—and that's OK! Just acknowledge the thoughts and bring your attention back to the phrase you will be repeating. It doesn't mean you are doing anything wrong.

Before we begin, think about your own personal spirituality. Think about what gives you meaning. You will need to select a word or a short phrase (up to about five words) that is meaningful and that you can repeat within the time it takes to exhale.

For example, if religious faith is significant and meaningful for you, you might wish to repeat part of a prayer. If nature holds deep meaning for you, you might want to repeat a word or phrase relating to nature or the Earth. Your meaningful phrase can relate to love, happiness, family, faith...or anything that is important to you.

You need to choose one word or one phrase and mentally repeat it during meditation. For example, you could use "Peace," "Love," "Serenity," or any other concept in the language of your religion.

To start, find a comfortable position. Small adjustments are OK, but try not to move around too much. The meditation you are about to do will take about five minutes. Keep your meaningful phrase in mind. I'll tell you when and how to repeat it.

Meditation

Close your eyes or focus your gaze on one small area. Start by relaxing your muscles. When thoughts arise, disregard them, thinking "hmm" or "oh well," and turn your attention back to your body.

Let your muscles become loose and relaxed, starting with your feet...your ankles.... lower legs...knees... upper legs...pelvis...torso...back...shoulders...arms... hands...face and head. Feel your body becoming loose and relaxed...

Turn your attention now to your breathing. Notice each breath, without trying to change your breathing in any way....

Just observe....as thoughts arise, acknowledge them and let them go, returning your attention to your breathing....breathe naturally....slowly..

As your thoughts wander, simply return your attention to your breathing. Notice your breath as it flows gently in and out of your body....without any effort....

Acknowledge your thoughts and focus again on your breathing. Interruptions are normal...just let these thoughts go and return your attention to your breathing. Now think of the meaningful word or phrase you selected...and say this word or phrase in your mind as you exhale. Each time you breathe out, say the word or the phrase. As your thoughts wander, bring your attention again to repeating your meaningful statement with each outward breath. Continue repeating the word or phrase each time you exhale.

Bring your attention back to the word or phrase you are repeating with each gentle breath out. With passive acceptance, continue to focus on the word or phrase, repeating it each time you breathe out... allowing distracting thoughts to float by.

Closing

Now slowly begin to reawaken. Turn your attention to your breathing. Notice your calm, smooth breaths... in and out. Allow your awareness to turn now to your body...calm and relaxed. Notice how your body feels...become more aware of your surroundings.

Now let your attention turn to your thoughts... back to normal conscious awareness. Sit quietly for a moment with your eyes open...enjoy the feeling of relaxation while gradually re-awakening. Adjust your position slightly.

Reflect upon the experience of meditation. Notice what it was like...notice how you feel now...free from worries about how well you did...knowing that whatever happened was the correct and natural response.

Wiggle your fingers and toes...roll your shoulders...stretch if you like...and when you are ready, begin your mindful prayer.

CHAPTER 3

Applying Mindfulness to Prayer

The concept of mindfulness has been around for quite a while, but applying it to the experience of prayer is a relatively new concept that actually makes a lot of sense. Let's explore how we can apply mindfulness to the goal of mindful prayer.

Being fully present

One of the core principles of mindfulness is being fully present. This requires you to focus on what you are trying to accomplish with your prayers, and to realize that you are attempting to engage in a deep spiritual experience. Being fully present calls for being in the moment, which means trying to let go of baggage from the past or worries about the future. It allows you to experience the silence of being in the present without the noise of distractions that prevent you from focusing on meaningful prayer.

EXERCISE 5:
ACHIEVING THE EXPERIENCE
OF BEING FULLY PRESENT

Observing your thoughts and feelings without judgment

Another core idea behind the concept of mindfulness is letting go of judgment, especially as it relates to our thoughts and feelings. Getting caught up in what we are thinking or feeling when we want to pray can keep us from fully engaging in the experience. If we are preoccupied with our thoughts or emotions about someone else, it is difficult to connect with God. For that matter, judging ourselves or others is really counterproductive to attaining a higher level of spiritual experience. It should be fairly obvious that judgment and connecting more deeply with our spiritual selves are mutually exclusive. It's impossible to achieve a deep spiritual connection if you're busy judging your thoughts and feelings.

Similarly, you can't expect to achieve mindful prayer while you are judging someone you believe has wronged you or while focusing on their flaws. It just doesn't work. So, letting go of judgment, acknowledging what you are experiencing and feeling, and accepting the imperfect people in your life will undoubtedly help you create space for a more mindful and ultimately more effective prayer experience.

> Wherever you are, just stop and look around when safe to do so. Become aware of everything that your senses pick up. Focus on what you are hearing, what you are feeling, what you are smelling, maybe even what you're tasting. Ask yourself: "What am I feeling right now?" Are you feeling relaxed, joyful, or inquisitive? Do you feel over-stimulated or anxious? Are feeling sad or lonely? Then, ask yourself the simple question, "Where am I?" And answer with "I am here." This may help you to feel fully present in the moment, and bring—acceptance to where and who you are.

Meta-cognition

Meta-cognition, which loosely translates as thinking about one's thinking, is a key concept behind letting go of our thoughts. Most often, we allow ourselves to think without considering the impact of our thought patterns.

Meta-cognition is a foundational principle of cognitive psychology, based on the idea that our thoughts affect our emotions, which in turn directly affect our behavior. The primary step toward letting go of these impediments that block the ability to pray mindfully is being aware of our judgmental thoughts, whether toward ourselves or others. If you aren't monitoring your thoughts, you won't know if they are toxic and preventing you from praying effectively, and you won't know if you need to let them go. Once you engage in meta-cognition and monitor your thoughts, you will become aware of judgments, which enables you to set them aside.

EXERCISE 6A:
LETTING GO OF SELF-JUDGMENTS

If you find yourself focusing on your flaws or past mistakes while trying to pray, try coming up with a phrase that helps you accept your flaws or forgive yourself for what you may have done that was harmful or immature. Consider these options:

"I am human, so I am, of course, flawed like everyone else, and that's OK. Now is not the time to focus on that. Now is the time to turn to God."

"God, help me to accept myself just as I am, and help me to improve and to work on myself and my flaws."

"God, please help me to become a better version of myself."

EXERCISE 6B:
LETTING GO OF JUDGMENTS OF OTHERS

If you find yourself focusing on judging other people while trying to engage in prayer, create a phrase that allows you to let go of these judgments and refocus on your ability to pray mindfully. Consider these options:

"I am flawed, too, and no better than anyone else. So, help me let go of these judgments about other people and focus instead on asking God to help me work on my own flaws."

"Help me stop judging him/her and just accept things as they are, so I can focus on connecting with God."

"This is not the time to focus on judging. This is the time to connect with the true judge, God."

Cultivating a deeper connection with God

Mindfulness can also help us establish a deeper connection with God or whatever Higher Power we are trying to reach. It allows for a more focused, purposeful experience that can ultimately lead to a greater feeling of connectedness in general. Prayer is a means by which we can achieve that spiritual connection. Being more mindful of that goal when we pray can actually help facilitate it.

Remember that the ultimate goal of prayer is to achieve a deeper connection with God. Focusing on that goal by being more mindful of it even before beginning to pray will help us achieve that deeper connection. (The next chapter offers a more thorough discussion of intention.)

You may also need to work on connecting more deeply with yourself in order to achieve a deeper connection with God. Those of us who are emotionally disconnected in general, and are not connected with ourselves, may find it more difficult to connect spiritually. Yet, in order to connect with others, you need to be connected with yourself.

If you are concerned about being internally disconnected, consider working with a good psychodynamic therapist who can help you uncover the reasons why you may not be connecting with yourself emotionally and help you find ways to become more emotionally connected. If you can accomplish that, it may help you become more spiritual and more connected with God through prayer.

Achieving calmness and serenity

It is difficult to imagine being unsettled, nervous, and anxious while, at the same time, being spiritually connected. The two realities just don't seem to go together. Spirituality and mindful prayer truly require a certain degree of calmness and serenity. These seem to be the basic prerequisites for achieving a true spiritual connection. However, prayer can also be a route to achieving calmness and serenity, if you can ease yourself enough to try.

If you refer to the exercises in Chapter 2, including anchoring, breathing, and meditation, you will find some excellent ways to deal with being distracted by anxiety or worry. Using these techniques can help reduce or even eliminate stimuli that are keeping you from praying mindfully and effectively. Also, bilateral stimulation, which is used in Eye Movement Desensitization and Reprocessing (EMDR), discussed in detail in Chapter 6, can be quite effective in calming the nervous system and helping you prepare for mindful prayer.

I recently conducted an EMDR training session for therapists in Israel, as part of my volunteer activities in an effort to help that traumatized nation. One of the participants was a therapist and a unique rabbi who is wildly popular due to his innovative programs and prayer experiences. He reported during the training that he regularly engages his congregants in calming and "connecting" preparation exercises before prayer to help them be more mindful and effective. Each morning, he leads an exercise in meditation, breathing, self-hypnosis, or centering (e.g. anchoring) to help them become more mindful and focused during prayer. As a result of the EMDR training, he reported back to us that he is also introducing bilateral stimulation prior to prayer services to help reduce the overactivation of the limbic system, the emotional part of the brain, and to calm the nervous system in general to facilitate a more serene prayer experience.

Using natural remedies to achieve calmness and serenity

In addition, you may also want to consider some natural agents that can help you calm down before trying to pray. Many of my patients have found these naturopathic remedies to be extremely effective in calming an overly activated nervous system, allowing them to focus on mindful prayer with a more settled and serene mindset. These remedies include:

➤ **Valerian root**—This herb is often used as a natural sleep agent, but with anxious people, it can be highly effective in reducing anxiety and achieving a greater sense of relaxation and calmness. The only real drawback to valerian root is that it tastes pretty awful, but if you can tolerate it, or drink some juice afterward to dilute the flavor, it can really affect your ability to manage your anxiety with little to no risk or side effects. I have found that the liquid form of valerian root is much more effective than the capsule form, because it is purer, since the capsules contain various fillers and solidifying agents. If you ingest the liquid sublingually, under the tongue, it enters the bloodstream directly, as opposed to capsules, which must first be digested through the gastrointestinal system before being absorbed.

➤ **Kava**—This herb can also help reduce anxiety and achieve a deeper sense of calm. It is basically tasteless and therefore easier to tolerate. The only possible concern is that there have been some reports, although quite rare, of kidney damage in people who used large amounts of kava over long periods of time. However, most research studies have deemphasized this risk, suggesting that moderate, periodic use of kava—for example, to enhance calmness before prayer—should carry no risk of future medical issues. It is also available in liquid form, which, again, is preferable to the capsule form.

➤ **Amino acids**—There is widespread evidence that certain amino acids, such as l-theanine and l-tryptophan (which is found at high levels in turkey), can promote sleep for people who have difficulty falling asleep at night. However, for those who struggle with anxiety, these amino acids can also help reduce anxious feelings and induce a sense of calm. I recently discovered that both are available in liquid form containing helpful herbs, such as ginseng, ashwagandha, and ginkgo. The combination of the amino acids L-lysine and L-arginine have also been found to be very effective in reducing stress and anxiety and calming the nervous system.

➤ **Flowers**—Certain flowers seem to be able to calm a "nervous nervous system." They have also been found to be somewhat effective in inducing sleep for people who experience insomnia. The best-known of these flowers is chamomile, a mild, pleasant-tasting flower that is made into a tea, either on its own or with other flowers that have similar calming effects, such as lavender, elderflower, and passionflower.

Those of you whose anxiety is so intense that none of these methods prove effective may wish to consider a consultation with a psychiatrist to see if any medication could help get your anxiety under control. I am not a huge fan of resorting to medications when psychological treatments can often be equally effective, but there are times that medications may be necessary when all else fails and the anxiety is severe or disabling.

However, I strongly urge you to try non-benzodiazepine medications first. Examples include Selective Serotonin Reuptake Inhibitor (SSRI) medications like Prozac, Zoloft, and Luvox. The latter specifically targets anxiety symptoms related to Obsessive-Compulsive Disorder (OCD). Wellbutrin or Effexor are also known to help with anxiety. These medications do not have much, if any, potential for addiction, are usually not sedating, and can be withdrawn rather effectively over time. However, typical benzodiazepine anti-anxiety medications such as Xanax, Valium, and Ativan have a high potential for addiction, are sedating, and often pose difficulties in terms of withdrawal. I generally do not advise using these medications unless the anxiety is severe and it is absolutely necessary, and then only periodically and for shorter periods of time.

Regardless of the method you choose to achieve calmness and serenity to enhance your prayer experience, please try to be consistent in using it. Praying while calm and relaxed helps you connect more deeply with your spirituality and ultimately with your Creator.

Mantras

Unlike the longer phrases offered in Exercise 6 above, mantras or shorter phrases and simple words can help redirect our attention away from negative or self-sabotaging thoughts, perhaps even more effectively. Over time, mantras can actually break down old, dysfunctional neural pathways that create negative patterns of thinking and install new neural pathways. This helps eliminate negativity or anxiety and induces a greater sense of calm and serenity that can greatly enhance your prayers.

EXERCISE 7: CREATING OR CHOOSING MANTRAS

Try to come up with a mantra or several mantras that you can use to prepare for prayer and help yourself become more calm, serene, and engaged before initiating actual prayer.

Alternatively, choose among these options. Remember that you don't have to use the same mantra each time, although some people prefer to just repeat the same mantra for familiarity's sake, feeling that it helps establish a specific positive neural pathway:

Words:

"Calm"   "Focus"

"Relax"   "Connect"

"Soothe"

Short phrases:

"Stay calm"   "Let it be"

"Time to connect"   (especially if you are

"Find your center"   a Beatles fan...)

"Let it go"

Using a mantra before prayer can be quite effective in enhancing your experience and achieving the ultimate goal of connecting with God on a regular basis.

Visualizations

Some of us are more cognitive in the way we experience the world. We are thinkers who spend a great deal of time engaged in deep thought, processing our experiences cognitively in order to connect spiritually. For such thinkers, prayer and spirituality are more rational because belief in God makes sense to us. Therefore, it makes sense to pray to God in the belief that He created the world and continues to create and influence our day-to-day lives.

Other people are more emotional in the way that they connect spiritually and experience deeply felt emotions that influence the depth of their spirituality. Still others connect behaviorally through daily rituals of keeping the commandments, giving charity, helping the poor, or volunteering at activities sponsored by their house of worship.

Some of us, however, are more visual in the way we experience the world, and we can use this sense to guide us to a more spiritual experience. For us, visualizing God's creations, or allowing the viewing of things we see in our everyday lives to enrich our spirituality, leads to a deeper spiritual experience. Visual people experience God and spirituality by observing inspiring things in nature: a rainbow after a storm, intense cloud formations, a field of beautiful flowers, majestic mountains, the vastness of the ocean, the dramatic effect of a waterfall, or the stillness of a calm lake. Those who experience the world more visually can use visualization to inspire more meaningful prayer.

Even those who are more cognitive, emotional, or

behavioral in their approach to spirituality can still try to use visualizations before prayer to help them make the transition from the hectic pace of their lives or their stressful thoughts to a calmer, more connected prayer experience. Unless you generally have difficulty visualizing, which can happen, try using visualization techniques for a few seconds before praying. This will help you disconnect from the daily intensity of your life and connect with the serenity of mindful prayer.

EXERCISE 8:
USING VISUALIZATIONS BEFORE PRAYER

Before praying, choose an image that calms your nervous system. Now focus on it briefly—or for as long as you need to make the transition from an experience of stress or intensity toward a calmer, more relaxed frame of mind—as a path toward achieving more meaningful, mindful prayer. Take as little or as much time as you feel you need to achieve this transition, or whenever you feel that you are ready to begin praying more mindfully. Here are some examples of images that may be helpful:

- Lying on a beach looking out toward the ocean as the sun is setting

- Standing on top of a mountain looking out toward the mountain range

- Lounging lazily in a boat in the middle of a lake

- Experiencing the stillness of being in the middle of the woods

- Peering down at a little child sleeping in his or her crib

- Being in your grandmother's arms

- Seeing any image that represents God for you

CHAPTER 4

Intentionality

Origins of Intentionality

The concept of intentions is not new, at least not to me. I was introduced to it as a result of my work with psychedelic-supported psychotherapy in 2023. I had been working, rather unsuccessfully I might add, with a young patient who was unable to overcome a rather severe addiction, even though both of us put forth a tremendous amount of effort to deal with the problem. All of the tricks that I had in my bag of therapy tools were ineffective in helping him overcome the compulsion to act out, and inpatient treatment was not an option for him.

He approached me with the idea of using psychedelics to help him get the problem under control, because a friend of his with a similar problem had experienced great success with this treatment. An intense psychotherapy intervention using psilocybin mushrooms, also referred to as "magic mushrooms," rather dramatically stopped his friend from continuing to act out.

As someone who considers himself fairly conservative and who avoids any mind-altering substances, I found the idea quite off-putting at first. I don't even drink alcohol, except for religious ceremonial purposes, and when I do imbibe, it's usually a low-alcohol wine variant (just a notch above sparkling grape juice). I am just not comfortable with anything that affects my ability to stay focused and stable. I also had been conditioned to believe that any illegal drug is just plain 'bad,' and the idea of being involved in any such thing caused me significant discomfort.

My patient was persistent and proceeded to send me a flurry of articles that described strong research being conducted at highly credible institutions of higher education, such as Johns Hopkins University, New York University, and the University of California-Davis. Their studies found clear evidence of the therapeutic effects of psychedelic substances, such as psilocybin mushrooms, LSD, MDMA, and ketamine, which showed significant positive impact on addiction, as well as trauma, depression, and anxiety, when facilitated properly.

The positive effects were seen mostly within structured psychotherapy, using psychedelic medicines to enhance the therapeutic process. Conceptually, it is seen as producing greater neuroplasticity in the brain. This allows for greater openness and confers the ability to reexperience traumas and negative experiences in ways that can be reframed so they contribute to enhanced healing. Results from random, controlled trials have shown significant reduction in trauma symptoms and addictive behaviors, as well as improvements in depression and anxiety.

The process involves three stages:

1. **Intentions**—Identifying the goals that the patient wishes to achieve allows for the development of specific neural pathways through which the medicine can travel. That can help achieve the patient's goals, as opposed to a random trip that has no specific goals.

2. **The actual journey**—The patient experiences the psychedelic agent with the assistance of a trained, experienced facilitator along with a licensed therapist who assists in the process.

3. **Integration**—The patient integrates the psychedelic experience with the previously outlined intentions and identifies ways that the process can help him or her achieve those identified goals.

The first stage, intention, is our focus for this chapter. I have adopted the concept of intentionality for use in psychotherapy and have advised my patients to focus each morning on their intentions in terms of their therapeutic goals. This has proven to be a powerful catalyst for achieving those goals, so it makes intuitive sense to apply it also to the goal of praying mindfully.

Preparing for Prayer

Using intentions to prepare for prayer is not a new concept. As mentioned earlier, in Judaism, *"hitbodedut"* is an intense communication with God that involves deeply felt emotions and a review of what you want to express to Him. It precedes the actual prayer service and helps a person prepare for a more personal prayer experience.

Similarly, by identifying and explicitly expressing our intentions before we pray, we can clearly set the tone for a more mindful, purposeful experience. We can also reduce the possibility of our prayers being automatic or less mindful.

Psychological research has shown that preparing for an experience tends to enhance its effect, as opposed to going through it without any preparation. Spontaneity can be a positive means of experiencing many aspects of life, like sports, recreation, and entertainment. However, when it comes to experiences that carry a lot of meaning and require a greater amount of concentration and depth, it seems obvious that mindful preparation through the use of intentions would greatly enhance the experience's positive impact.

In fact, some of the researchers of psychedelic treatment found that going through psychedelic-supported therapy with stated intentions resulted in far greater therapeutic progress than just experiencing it without intentionality preceding the intervention. It can therefore be extrapolated that using intentions can lead to a deeper, more meaningful prayer experience.

EXERCISE 9: USING INTENTIONS BEFORE PRAYER

Prepare a list of intentions, or the goals you would like to accomplish through prayer. Try to make it as comprehensive as possible. Then, each morning or evening (or both, if you pray both in the morning and evening), choose an intention that you wish to focus on and use that intention to prepare before praying.

Here are a few examples of intentions on which you may wish to focus:

- Serenity

- Health for yourself or a loved one

- Getting closer to God

- Increasing your spirituality

- Sustenance/livelihood

- Overcoming sin

- Controlling unhealthy behavior

- Getting closer to your spouse

- Having more patience for your children

- Others?

Before praying, focus on the intention you have chosen. Try to hold onto that thought alone, excluding any other thoughts that may creep into your consciousness at that moment. Develop a clear vision of what you want to achieve through praying regarding that intention. Feel free to choose any of these possibilities, or come up with your own intention, something specific that works for you. The important thing is to be consistent in using an intention before praying, so that you maximize the possibility of having an effective and meaningful prayer experience.

Expectancy Effect

There is also the possibility of a positive expectancy effect, which makes it more likely that you will achieve what you intended to accomplish. The expectancy effect, a concept that originated in cognitive psychology, posits that if you expect something to happen, it's more likely to occur.

Conversely, if you expect something not to happen, it's more likely *not* to happen. So, if you tend to be a more negativistic or pessimistic person, and you assume that good things won't happen, then it's more than likely that you won't be as effective in praying. If you are generally pessimistic, you may want to challenge your negative assumptions, and at least try to use some of the tools that we are presenting, while assuming that they will work for you. You have nothing to lose but your negativity (for more discussion about this, see Chapter 5).

You will find that preparing for prayer, whether through applying your intentions or any other method that works for you, will greatly enhance your prayer experience. Intentions give you a "leg up" in praying mindfully.

Sharpening focus

Using intentions to pray more mindfully can help you sharpen your focus on the task at hand. This is better than allowing your mind to wander to your to-do list, events of the day, or other unrelated issues that keep you from focusing on connecting with your Higher Power.

Many people, including myself, find it challenging to stay focused while praying. Allowing yourself to focus on what you intend to accomplish through prayer can actually help you stay more focused while praying. When you set your intentions prior to beginning to pray, you are orienting yourself to the focus of connecting through prayer, and that can only benefit the entire experience.

Intentionality can be a powerful tool for gaining control of your wandering mind and keeping focused on what you are praying about. Whether you pray to feel more spiritually connected, to pray for yourself or a loved one, or to pray for peace in the world, setting those intentions can help you stay focused and feel more fulfilled. Imagine the satisfaction of knowing that you accomplished what you set out to do, and did not allow yourself to get distracted and go to places in your mind that take you away from your goal of connecting.

Developing new neural pathways

Our brains are wired so that established neurological connections, or neural pathways, develop over time. These connections steer us toward certain patterns of thinking or behaving.

The saying "neurons that are wired together fire together" is a way of explaining this phenomenon, which helps us understand that our patterns are wired by previous experiences that create these neural pathways.

In many ways, the goal of psychotherapy is to create neural pathways that reflect a more reality-based way of seeing things or more adaptive modes of thinking. This can help us think, feel, and function better. Similarly, by using intentions to set the stage for mindfulness while praying, you establish new neural pathways that can help you develop new patterns of focus and intention, thus facilitating more effective and meaningful prayer.

At a broader, more macro level, using intentions to develop new neural pathways can also give us a greater sense of agency or mastery over our thoughts and allow us to feel that we are in control, rather than letting our thoughts control us. This can be a powerful tool for everyone, especially those with clinically diagnosed conditions that prevent them from functioning at a higher level in general and hampers them from being the best versions of themselves. In the next chapter, we will address various issues that can keep us from being mindful in general and from engaging in mindful prayer specifically.

CHAPTER 5

Impediments to Mindful Prayer

Now that we have talked about how to enhance your experience of prayer and how to be more mindful while praying, we will turn to some issues that may impede your ability to have a positive prayer experience. Since this book is intended to be a more clinical discussion of mindful prayer, it makes sense to address the factors that make it difficult for people to achieve a meaningful prayer experience.

The following issues can be impediments to mindful prayer:

Obsessive thinking

There is a neurocognitive reality that we can't think two thoughts simultaneously. Our brains are wired to allow us to focus on only one thought at a time. Unfortunately, when our mind is preoccupied with a flurry of obsessive thoughts, it is impossible to focus on more meaningful things that can lead to mindful prayer. People formally diagnosed with Obsessive-Compulsive Disorder (OCD) are seriously challenged by obsessive thinking that they can't control. These obsessions can literally take over their minds, causing them to become preoccupied with their obsessive thoughts. They literally have no ability to control them, and this creates a great deal of stress and anxiety.

As a result, people with OCD often struggle with their ability to pray. It's difficult to focus on your prayers if your head is filled with competing thoughts that are out of control, distressing, and distracting. OCD is considered an anxiety disorder and, as such, it can really interfere with people's ability to emotionally connect with their spirituality. It's obviously difficult to have a positive spiritual experience when you are filled with anxiety, worry, or nervousness.

You don't need to have OCD to struggle with obsessive thoughts. I personally have the tendency to get involved in my head a lot (after all, I am a psychologist...), and even though I don't have OCD, per se, I tend to struggle to get out of my head and into my heart. This often interferes with my ability to connect emotionally during my daily prayer rituals. This challenge was actually the main impetus for writing this book, because I know that if I struggle with this challenge, many people may have the same difficulty and could benefit from helpful tools and suggestions.

CASE HISTORY 1: SHARON

Sharon* is a middle-aged professional who grew up in a traditional, observant Jewish household. Daily prayer, whether at home or in the synagogue, was an expected and important part of her life. However, because the home she grew up in was also rather chaotic and unstable, she developed serious symptoms of OCD. Sharon's OCD compensated for her disordered upbringing and manifested primarily through obsessive thinking. This resulted in her inability to sustain concentration and focus on pretty much anything other than the latest worry or task that needed to be done. Consequently, prayer was an extremely challenging experience for her, because her mind routinely wandered in multiple directions, focusing on a wide variety of issues in the past or worries about the future—anything but the prayers she was reading in her prayer book.

She came in for treatment because, as an educational administrator, she needed to be able to complete tasks on time and to manage her staff. This required her to be focused and task-oriented. However, because of her OCD, she found that her perfectionism interfered with getting things done in a timely fashion, and her supervisory role was causing her tremendous anxiety because she feared her staff or her board would judge her if she made a mistake or didn't meet their expectations as a leader.

As we explored how her OCD symptoms affected other areas of her life, Sharon confided in me that one of the most distressing aspects of the disorder was that it caused her to be completely incapable of focusing during prayers. Instead, her mind would wander incessantly to random worries or obsessions about her job, and that interfered with her ability to connect to her prayers.

We explored different treatment options, and she decided that she would try a combination of psychiatric medication, cognitive therapy, and psychodynamic therapy to explore the underpinnings of the disorder and how her upbringing contributed to her perfectionism and obsessive thinking.

She made an appointment with a psychiatrist who prescribed Luvox, an SSRI medication that targets OCD symptoms, along with Buspar to help control her anxiety. Sharon also learned cognitive therapy techniques such as "thought stopping," which can help reduce obsessive thinking and stop unwanted rumination that interferes with daily living, as well as prayer. She also took up yoga and began a daily exercise routine that produced a significant centering effect on her mind and body. She found that the weekly therapeutic massages and acupuncture that I recommended calmed her body and nervous system, which helped with the OCD, as well.

Finally, she learned to initiate deep breathing and focused intentions before prayer, and that helped her prepare herself to be calmer and more mindful when praying. She found that having clear intentions helped her be more mindful of the goal of becoming more immersed in prayer. This was a significant contrast to her previous state of being cognitively out of control, with her mind wandering aimlessly to any of a variety of distressing topics. She actually found intentionality most useful in helping her stay focused and mindful while praying, instead of her usual pattern of being highly distracted and unable to focus.

As a result of all of her work, she reported that, for the first time, she was able to pray in a way that she had never experienced before. As a result of her mindful prayer, she was able to tap into a much deeper spiritual self. For Sharon, this was an incredible gift that enabled her to connect to God and the spirituality she had longed for, but that her OCD had blocked.

Attention deficits

The ability to pray mindfully depends, to a large extent, on your ability to focus and keep your attention on the prayers you are offering. To pray effectively, you must have the ability to focus on your prayers, instead of allowing your wandering eye to focus on everything except the prayer book. In Judaism, it is strongly recommended that you use a prayer book for all prayers, even if you know them by heart. That may seem nonsensical to you, and the truth is that I often find it difficult to discipline myself to read from my prayer book when engaged in the prayers I know by heart. However, I have found that my mind is much more likely to wander when I pray with my eyes closed than when I force myself to read from my prayer book. This is because I am much less likely to be distracted by random thoughts or external stimuli when I focus on reading the prayer than when I pray by heart.

The challenge of focusing while praying is especially difficult for people who are formally diagnosed with Attention Deficit Disorder (ADD). This is especially the case if they have hyperactive ADD, or ADHD. People with this disorder find it particularly hard to focus or pay attention to things that aren't very motivating or stimulating, because their brains are wired in such a way that they are generally more easily distracted and unfocused. This is primarily due to deficits in the frontal lobe, which regulates "executive functions." These include a wide range of capabilities, such as organizational skills, time and space management, task completion, and judgment. All of these skills are important for managing your life. Perhaps attention and focus are the most important executive functions in relation to our discussion.

Although attention and focus are related concepts, there are subtle differences between the two. The ability to attend to something means paying attention when someone is speaking to you, following the thread of a discussion, or being attentive to the feelings and needs of another person. Focusing is more about zeroing in on what you are reading or on a detail you need to track, without allowing yourself to be distracted. This is more of a micro-level function that requires the ability to sustain focus over a period of time in order to accomplish your goal.

The truth is that mindful prayer requires both attention and focus. We need to sustain our focus on our prayer book to keep track of the prayers and not allow ourselves to drift away from that focus. We also, however, need to stay attentive to the emotional and spiritual aspects of the experience at a more macro level, in order to more fully appreciate it. People with ADD or ADHD clearly have more difficulty staying focused on their prayers and on the spiritual aspects of the experience.

CASE HISTORY 2: ERIC

For Eric, life had always been a challenge. Although he was bright and personable, he struggled quite a bit in school, had difficulty paying attention, and got in trouble for impulsive and aggressive behavior. He went to a parochial school, and although it was very hard for him to sit still and focus during class, it was nearly impossible during religious services. That's when he was more likely to act up and get in trouble because the teachers perceived his disruptive behavior as disrespectful.

Somehow, his ADHD was not diagnosed until he got to college, so no one understood the underlying dynamics of his behavioral and attention difficulties during his childhood and teenage years. As a result,

he was labeled a "difficult kid," and his teachers con-
cluded that punishment was the only way to deal with
him. Of course, he generally associated school and
religion with resentment, frustration, and negative
experiences. Once he left his home for college, he
abandoned any real involvement with his family's religious observance.

For a period of time, Eric had no interest in his religion or any spiritual experience. Then, during his junior
year, he met a girl who was deeply involved in a religious
organization on campus. She encouraged him to join her
for a holiday dinner, and then a class, and, eventually, a
prayer service. His experience there was vastly different from the rote, monotonous services that he remem-
bered from his childhood. He really enjoyed being a part
of the college organization. He met other students who
had gotten into the "whole religion thing" on campus,
and he embraced the experience, especially since his
new love interest, Jamie, was heavily involved.

As much as he was enjoying his overall involvement with the organization, his ability to sustain attention and focus during the prayer services remained
a problem. He was frustrated when he saw his peers
enthusiastically singing and getting into the services,
while he couldn't keep up because of his distractibility. He would constantly look around the room, seeing
what other people were doing, instead of reading the
prayer book and participating in the service. He knew

that being able to focus and sustain attention was a problem for him, since a student health center physician had diagnosed his ADHD during his first year in college. However, Eric never felt comfortable with the idea of taking medication. That is, until we met.

Eric came in to see me because a fellow student with ADHD had seen me for several years and found that the treatment had helped him get through college and manage his life better. Eric's primary reason for coming in was that he felt his ADHD was interfering with his ability to study and turn in assignments on time, which was greatly affecting his grades. Since he hoped to get into an MBA program, he decided to follow his friend's advice and come in for help, and Jamie encouraged him.

Although our primary focus was on how ADHD was affecting Eric's academic performance, at one point, he parenthetically mentioned to me that it was also affecting his ability to focus during the prayer services he had started to attend. This was important to him because Jamie was very much into it, and he wanted to share her enthusiasm, but his frustration was getting in the way.

When I asked him what he had been doing about his ADHD issue, he really couldn't come up with anything substantive. When I asked about medication, he told me that he "wasn't into the meds thing," and he didn't want "to be addicted to drugs." I assured him that

ADHD medications aren't really addictive. I explained that they could actually help his brain function by stimulating the frontal lobe, which regulates executive functions, such as organizational abilities, attention, focus, time management, and task completion.

I also asked him a hypothetical question: If he had been diagnosed with diabetes and required insulin, would he also say he "wasn't into the meds thing," or would he take it to stabilize and function properly? Of course, he said yes, he would take it—so I explained that ADHD medication is similar in that it helps the brain function normally and can improve all the areas that are problematic for people with ADHD. He agreed to at least give it a try. We also worked on other techniques, such as anchoring, intentions, and deep breathing before praying, which would hopefully help him be more focused and mindful during services.

A month later, Eric came back and told me that not only was his academic performance improving, but his ability to pray was greatly enhanced, due to the medication and the techniques that we had worked on. He reported that the entire prayer experience had changed as a result. He was more focused and could keep track of the prayers. This made him feel much more spiritually connected, perhaps for the first time, and also much more connected to the other students, notably Jamie, because he finally felt like he was fully part of the spiritual and social experience.

Depression

People who are depressed often find it difficult to be spiritually connected and to engage in meaningful prayer. Their emotions tend to be shut down, along with their ability to connect both emotionally and spiritually. If it is a more biologically based depression, then the neurons necessary to actively engage in mindful prayer are just not functioning properly, and the person's ability to focus on anything is often impaired. In fact, I have often referred to depression as a form of attention deficit for that reason.

Moreover, people who are depressed lack the motivation and drive to accomplish much of anything, and often find themselves unable to complete important goals, much less to pray successfully. It's sad and ironic that mindful prayer—one thing that could inspire them and overcome their "funk"—eludes them because they just don't have the psychological ability or the emotional bandwidth to pray meaningfully. They often barely have the energy to get up in the morning, much less the ability to pray.

People who have dysthymia, a more chronic, sub-clinical form of depression, can be viewed as having a "depressive personality." They don't *get* depressed, they *are* just depressive in general. Dysthymic people are generally negativistic, pessimistic, and depleted. For them, the proverbial cup is always half-empty, rather than half-full. These people have often experienced a sad and depressive childhood, either due to abuse or neglect. Alternatively, they may have been raised by negative, dysthymic parents who modeled negativity and pessimism for them and that became absorbed into their own personalities.

It's not hard to see why dysthymic people find it difficult to engage in anything spiritual, especially something so esoteric and potentially uplifting as prayer. Their often cynical attitudes toward anything religious tends to prevent them from being open to concepts such as God, religious rituals, or spirituality. Their negativistic attitudes, in general, keep them from exploring anything that could possibly be uplifting or inspiring. They just can't attach to anything that could be positive, and they sabotage any possibilities for increased happiness or meaning in their lives. For them, it's all a bunch of "stuff."

CASE HISTORY 3: CARL

A few years before Carl entered my office for the first time, his beloved wife Diane had passed away after a long fight against breast cancer. They had been married for more than 40 years and had a close, loving relationship. Carl had also recently retired, and he found that whatever meaning his life had held was gone. He had become severely depressed. In addition to losing his wife and his role as a dentist, he had also stopped going to church. As a devout Catholic, services had been an important part of his life with Diane, but going alone was too painful for him. When he tried, he couldn't concentrate on the prayers at all. He could only think about how much he had lost and how empty his life seemed.

Carl was clearly depressed, and the symptoms had affected his ability to have any sort of meaningful experience at Mass. Because of his intense sadness, he had difficulty focusing and was easily distracted, making any attempt at mindful prayer impossible. He eventually stopped going to church altogether because the entire experience was too painful and frustrating.

We first discussed trying an antidepressant medication, as well as a mild stimulant, to jumpstart his recovery and to allow for a boost of serotonin that could activate his brain and cognitive functioning. This could also help with his focus and concentration.

Additionally, I encouraged him to hire a trainer who would force him to get out of the house and do some exercise. Exercise often helps stimulate the production of endorphins, which can improve mood and energy level. We also did two sessions of EMDR to help desensitize the trauma of losing his wife, and to alleviate the intensity of the sadness and hopelessness he was feeling. Additionally, I arranged for him to meet with a Catholic priest I know at a nearby church. He is very welcoming and adept at working with complex emotions. He is also effective at inviting people who have left the church to return, and he persuaded Carl to come to Mass.

The relief from the depression and trauma due to the medication and EMDR, combined with the connection he made with the priest, enabled Carl to return to the church. He was surprised to see that his old ability to join in the prayers had come back as a result of all of the interventions he worked through. He also found that the ability to pray and reconnect spiritually was instrumental in alleviating his depression and enabling him to find new meaning in his life.

Narcissism—Anger/Resentment

When one thinks of narcissism in lay terms, what usually comes to mind is selfishness or self-centeredness. It is true that those issues are key components of that type of personality. However, narcissism has other aspects that relate to the discussion of impediments to mindful prayer.

Narcissists tend to be arrogant, judgmental, and lacking in humility. They can convince themselves that religious practices are archaic and outdated, and that only more primitive, unintelligent people engage in them. However, it is certainly the case that "religious" people of any persuasion can also be narcissistic, although, quite often, they aren't truly spiritual, and their ability to give themselves over to any sort of meaningful prayer is significantly limited. This is also the case because narcissists tend to resist any type of control, so they experience giving themselves over to a Higher Power as threatening because they don't want to be controlled or to give away their power to anyone, even to God.

As I wrote in my first book, *Breaking the Mirror—Overcoming Narcissism: How to Conquer Self-Centeredness and Achieve Successful Relationships*, "Quite often, narcissists have difficulty connecting spiritually because it requires an acknowledgment that there is something greater than you and that you're not omnipotent. This requires a degree of humility, an awareness that human beings are indeed not God, and that as humans we are quite imperfect, and in constant need of refinement and improvement. Spirituality enables us to look more deeply inside of ourselves, but narcissism often prevents us from doing so, because such introspection is too threatening for the fragile ego of a narcissist."

Ironically, while narcissism clearly impedes prayer and spirituality, prayer is precisely the activity that could help heal narcissism by facilitating a sense of deeper connection and humility. It is quite possible that someone who has narcissistic traits can find a way to connect through prayer and become a more humble, spiritual person. Also, the more mindful your prayer becomes, the deeper the connection with God. This can lead to greater spiritual development, even if you struggle with narcissistic traits.

CASE HISTORY 4: JULIE

Julie, a successful business owner in her early 40s, came in for therapy at the advice of her close friend, who had been my patient for a number of years. Julie had been divorced twice, and after her two failed marriages, she had suffered a more recent broken engagement. She was quite distraught since this pattern of unsuccessful relationships also extended to her two children, who had chosen to live with their dad instead of her.

Julie came from a highly demanding, critical family. Both of her parents were driven, ambitious people who expected a lot from their children, but gave them very little emotional support or validation. Based on her description of them, it would be fairly accurate to describe them as narcissistic, and it was equally clear that she was following in their footsteps.

However, instead of playing the role of the victim, as she apparently had been programmed to do throughout her life, this latest blow of losing her children forced her to face some painful realities about her own personality. Now she wanted to know how it had played a role in these failed relationships. She was finally able to face the fact that her demanding nature and lack of humility, as well as her focus on herself, had alienated pretty much everyone in her life.

I asked her to read my book, *Breaking the Mirror: Overcoming Narcissism,* and to come back with feedback about what she read that resonated with her, and what she actually wanted to work on as her therapeutic goals. When she returned, I asked her what she related to in the book. Quite dejectedly, she replied, "Pretty much everything." When I asked her to highlight three elements that stood out to her, she mentioned the impact of narcissism on relationships and the lack of empathy, which were fairly predictable. However, I didn't expect the third thing she brought up: her inability to feel any level of spiritual connection.

When I asked her what it was about that aspect that struck her, she replied that, being a member of a religious community, she always felt like an outlier because she didn't connect to the entire experience of being religious. She didn't like her church's rules and restrictions because they made her feel controlled; she felt that the religious girls she'd grown up with were "nerdy" and boring, and she couldn't connect at all to the prayer services.

I asked why she felt compelled to address that aspect of narcissism when she didn't relate to religion at all? Her reply helped me realize that she had more insight than I had understood, and that she was determined to break free from the pattern of self-centeredness and superficiality that had plagued her throughout her life. She had come to the realization that she had never been able to sustain any real relationship, so she decided to start by developing one with God. She was able to identify that perhaps her spiritual emptiness and inability to connect spiritually—the problem that had made her feel like such an outsider growing up—was a key factor in her inability to connect with other people in a healthy way.

This epiphany became a catalyst for a spiritual journey that she hoped would help her to transform herself from a self-involved, insensitive person into someone who was more mindful and effective in her relationships. I suggested that she find a spiritual mentor and take classes that focused on relationships and personal growth. She found a religious center that taught such classes and met with its spiritual leader. He agreed to work with her and help her achieve her goals.

She reported back to me that she was encouraged by what she found at the center, but she couldn't relate to the prayer service. She found the prayers rote and impersonal, and she couldn't connect to them at all. I suggested that she do an internet search for personal prayers that related directly to what she was trying to focus on. Then I suggested that she could create her own prayer service to use during services at the center or pray privately at home. We discussed preparing to pray by focusing on intentions and stating what she wanted to achieve through prayers. I asked her to imagine a dialogue with God that was more tailored and personal.

When she returned the next time, she was beaming and couldn't wait to report what she had achieved. She had found beautiful, creative prayers written by a contemporary writer, as well as a few Psalms that spoke to her. When she used them, she experienced emotionally moving praying for the first time in her life. Her ability to create a personal service and to prepare beforehand to focus on her goal of becoming a more humble, sensitive person helped her achieve a true spiritual connection.

This spiritual experience actually became a catalyst for a broader journey of personal growth that led her to take control of the narcissism in her personality and to be more mindful and effective in all relationships. This even extended to her parents, with whom she had always had a strained relationship. She started dating a man she met at the center and eventually married him. For the first time in her life, she was able to accomplish what had eluded her all those years—a successful, mutually gratifying relationship—and inner serenity.

Bipolar Disorder

Achieving a structured practice of mindful prayer generally requires an ability to adhere to some sort of schedule that includes time to pray. A number of religions have morning prayers as part of their daily ritual, as well as regimented times to pray throughout the day, to help them stay connected with God. If you find it difficult to remain emotionally or behaviorally stable, that obviously will affect your ability to maintain a routine of scheduled prayers.

Bipolar Disorder is a serious mental illness that causes extreme mood swings, ranging from severe depression to full-blown mania. At either extreme, it is difficult to conform to any schedule or regimen because your emotions can be overwhelming, even debilitating. As previously discussed, depression can shut down a person's ability to function in any capacity, making it quite difficult to have the energy or focus for any sort of meaningful prayer experience. Conversely, people who are manic can be so out of control and overly energized that their ability to sit still and engage in prayer is severely limited.

This is especially the case when the illness involves psychotic episodes, which is sometimes the case with Bipolar Disorder. When psychosis is involved, people are totally incapacitated and unable to function normally. Therefore, it is usually unrealistic to expect them to participate in any prayer service or pray privately. There are cases, however, in which people who are manic and psychotic can actually become hyper-religious and pray fervently, but this is generally not meaningful prayer. Instead, it is typically just a manifestation of the mania, in this instance involving intense spirituality, that will wane and usually disappear once the manic phase of the illness is over. It is really not a genuine expression of spiritual connection, but more of an unfortunate aspect of the illness that is related more to psychosis than spirituality.

Addictions

Addiction—whether related more to substances such as alcohol, painkillers, or cocaine, or to behaviors such as addiction to sex, shopping, or gambling—can greatly affect one's ability to connect spiritually and engage in effective prayer. Addictions can literally hijack a person away from any meaningful connection with a spouse, children, friends, or co-workers, as well as with prayer or God. Besides being obsessed with how to get the next "fix," the secretive nature of these addictions and the shame usually associated with them tend to keep people isolated and withdrawn from any intimate relationships. Unfortunately, this often applies to one's relationship with God as well.

It can be extremely difficult to maintain any spiritual connection when you are in the throes of an addiction, and, quite often, addicts leave the world of religious observance and prayer because their heads are mired elsewhere. The focus and behaviors associated with addiction are often incompatible with spirituality. This is especially true in the case of sex addiction, as its associated behaviors are highly incompatible with most religious values and beliefs.

People who are struggling with behavioral addictions are also often very depleted from related struggles and conflicts, as well as exhausted from running around to gambling halls, places to act out, or endless shopping sprees. It's difficult to imagine a situation in which someone who is heavily preoccupied with the need to feed an addiction would also have the headspace or emotional capacity to find a way to pray.

But, once again, the irony is that prayer is the very thing that could actually help the addict overcome this serious problem. There has been much research and clinical data showing that faith-based recovery programs tend to be more effective in helping people overcome their addictions than programs that are devoid of faith. The ability to pray to God for help in fighting this tough battle could be what helps people win, regain their sanity, and achieve the serenity they desperately want.

We'll talk more about spiritual counseling in the next chapter.

Trauma

Trauma is defined as a sudden, unexpected, or shocking event that affects an individual in varying ways that often have a strong impact over the long-term. Experiences such as domestic violence, child sexual abuse, assault, natural disasters, and infidelity or betrayal can all have lasting, debilitating effects. When the trauma develops into Post-Traumatic Stress Disorder (PTSD), a person's ability to concentrate, connect, or relate to anything spiritual can be greatly affected.

Many traumatized people I have worked with over the years lost their spiritual connection as a result of trauma. This has been especially true with betrayal trauma, as in the case of infidelity, domestic violence, or sexual abuse. A sense of betrayal can lead to feeling betrayed by God and questioning how He could allow such a thing to happen. This feeling may also arise from world events that cause widespread death and destruction, prompting the question, "Where was God?"

Traumatized people can also experience the kind of attention deficits we see in ADD, but their cause is fundamentally different. In contrast to ADD, which is usually caused by genetics or brain structure deficiencies, trauma affects the brain in other ways that involve flooding it with stress hormones such as cortisol, adrenaline, and noradrenaline. These hormones affect the functioning of neurotransmitters and neuroreceptor sites, which impact the brain's ability to focus and concentrate. Even though these causal factors are very different, the resulting symptoms are essentially the same. So, for trauma victims, the ability to focus on a prayer book or to concentrate on a specific prayer, can be greatly impaired.

Finally, as previously discussed within the context of narcissism and addictions, the ironic aspect of trauma is that it impedes the very thing that could be helpful in overcoming its devastating effects: a spiritual connection achieved through prayer. It is true that prayer, especially mindful and meaningful prayer, can help a person heal from trauma by reaching out to God for help. This can also help someone put things in perspective and recognize that it is, after all, God who runs the world.

CASE HISTORY 5: GREG

Having grown up in a completely secular family with no religious affiliation, Greg had no formal religious training and had never attended a prayer service in his life. However, that all changed when he was involved in a serious car accident, a head-on collision, which left him with serious physical injuries and a considerable amount of trauma. He ended up with his car wrapped around a tree. His friend, who had been in the passenger seat, was lying on the ground, unconscious from blunt trauma to his head. He ended up in a coma and eventually recovered consciousness, but suffered from symptoms of Traumatic Brain Injury (TBI) that continue to plague his life.

Understandably, Greg was consumed with guilt about his friend's condition. He was also experiencing rather severe symptoms of PTSD. Flashbacks and intrusive thoughts left him with distractibility and an inability to focus, which affected his capacity to function in a number of areas. After this unfortunate accident, a friend suggested he talk about his guilt with a minister his family knew. Greg went to meet with him and ended up developing a friendly relationship with the minister. When he invited Greg to a prayer service, he agreed to attend, although a bit reluctantly.

Greg was drawn to the stirring melodies of the prayers, the warmth of the people, and the minister's inspiring sermon. But, he was disturbed that the strong emotions elicited by the prayers and the minister's words triggered flashbacks and distressing, intrusive thoughts that prevented him from focusing for much of the time during the service. When he returned a second time, the flashbacks were even worse. He ended up leaving in the middle of the service, despondent and feeling hopeless about ever connecting spiritually, despite his intense desire to find spiritual comfort.

The first intervention we tried was EMDR to treat the trauma, and hopefully to cause the PTSD symptoms to diminish over time. Greg responded well to the treatment, and he reported that the images of the accident and his intense guilt about his friend's unfortunate situation had abated considerably as a result. Cognitive therapy helped reinforce the message from the EMDR treatment that the other driver had been at fault, and Greg's guilt was not reasonable or rational. I also suggested some natural calming agents to help generate a greater sense of calmness, which helped him stay focused and more relaxed.

Within a few weeks, Greg was ready to attend the prayer service again, but this time, he was much calmer and more focused. He reported that he was able to get through the service with ease, and that his praying was much more effective and mindful, resulting in a far more meaningful experience.

As a result of his new spiritual connection and the therapeutic interventions we worked on, Greg reported that his PTSD symptoms and pervasive guilt had all but disappeared, and he was ready to live life more fully. Instead of being plagued by strong negative emotions and flashbacks, he was filled with gratitude and inspired by his newfound faith. He had also met a woman who attended the same church and had started dating her. His life was becoming more complete and fulfilling.

CHAPTER 6

Solutions to Overcoming Impediments

If any of the above challenges to mindful prayer resonate with you, pay close attention to this chapter on solutions. Our focus is on solutions, not just the problems themselves. If you are serious about working on your ability to enhance your experience with prayer, carefully considering these suggestions will help you enormously.

The treatment options aren't listed in any particular order. Some will apply to a number of different impediments, whereas others may target a specific one. You will be more comfortable with some of these concepts than you are with others, but I invite you to explore and be open to all of them as possible options. You don't want to take on too many recommendations at first, because it may be overwhelming. Perhaps start with one or two, and then add others if it feels right for you. Some of you may be more comfortable with only one modality at a time, whereas the more adventurous may be willing to dive in and try a few. Before we get started, however, let me share a word regarding the concept of multi-modality.

Multi-modal Therapy

Psychologist Arnold Lazarus developed the concept of multi-modal therapy in the 1970s, as a reaction to the unidimensional approaches of psychoanalysis and behavior therapy. He challenged the field of psychology to be more holistic and client-centered. He urged practitioners to recognize that an individually tailored approach to therapy would be more effective than the more traditional one-therapy-fits-all approach because it allows for the inclusion of different modalities that reflect various aspects of a person's presenting problem. The multi-modal approach is designed to be both comprehensive and integrative, in that it attempts to address all aspects of an individual by synergistically interweaving eclectic approaches.

I have used this approach since the earliest years of my career, because the concept of being eclectic and integrative made more sense to me than a one-therapy strategy, given the complexities and multiple dimensions of my patients and their problems. I have also encouraged students and clinicians I have supervised and trained to adopt this model, and to get as much training as possible in a variety of modalities. This enables them to be flexible and address their clients' needs with a modality that fits their particular problem, as opposed to being trained in one theoretical orientation and applying it to all their patients. They have found the multi-modal approach to treatment highly effective, in that it enhances their ability to help their patients reach their therapeutic goals.

In the context of our discussion, once you have identified

the issues you need to work on to pray more mindfully, you may want to consider working with a more broadly trained therapist who has an eclectic approach to therapy, so you can see which modalities make sense for you. Remember that mindfulness involves different dimensions of your experience, including its cognitive, emotional, physiological, somatic, and spiritual aspects. Keep that in mind as you decide who you want to work with and what you want to do to accomplish your goals.

Psychotherapy

There are many different approaches to psychotherapy, but before we delve into them, let's examine what "psychotherapy" means. Essentially, it involves establishing a therapeutic relationship with a trained therapist whose role is to guide you through a process designed to help you achieve your therapeutic goals. How you get there greatly depends on the therapist's orientation.

In the most basic terms, psychoanalytically oriented therapists use classic Freudian concepts and techniques to help patients gain a deeper understanding of their personality dynamics. They work to understand the influences of their unconscious mind, and how those influences helped their symptoms develop. The therapy derives insights from intrapersonal conflicts and early family-of-origin dynamics that shaped the client.

Psychodynamic therapy is also an insight-oriented therapy, but it's less strictly Freudian. It focuses on the development of a deeper understanding of how symptoms and personality issues developed as a result of the client's earlier experiences.

Behavioral therapy is more goal-oriented. It targets measurable goals that address maladaptive behaviors that are adversely affecting one's life. It's based on the premise that if something can't be measured, it doesn't exist, which, on the one hand, makes things simpler and more focused. On the other hand, though, it ignores the complexities of inner thoughts and emotions that are not really measurable at all.

Cognitive therapy deals with distorted, irrational, or maladaptive thought patterns that lead to emotional and behavioral issues. It identifies and challenges these patterns and cognitive distortions and encourages and reinforces new, more reality-based thinking.

It is fundamentally based on the concept that our thoughts affect our feelings, which, in turn, affect our behavior. So, according to cognitive therapy, you can change the way you feel and react by monitoring and changing the way you think.

Cognitive-behavioral therapy combines behavioral and cognitive approaches, integrating both of these models to achieve measurable goals. It is a structured approach that helps individuals manage challenges by changing the way they think and behave. It focuses on concrete skills that help change negative and unhelpful thought and behavioral patterns, resulting in improved mood and overall well-being.

Mental health professionals also work with other, newer approaches such as mindfulness-based cognitive therapy, which incorporates mindfulness practices such as meditation, deep breathing, and awareness of the present moment. It also uses narrative therapy, which helps people rewrite their personal story in a way that is healing and empowering. We will discuss alternative approaches later in this chapter.

For the purpose of our discussion on mindful prayer, it is likely that cognitively focused psychological approaches would be the most efficient and effective, since we are trying to refocus our thoughts on a deeper prayer experience. Using therapy to gain more control of our thought patterns and to become more focused and mindful, can go a long way in helping us achieve a higher level of prayer.

However, if you are unable to pray mindfully due to complex family or personal issues, you may find that some other psychotherapy approaches are more beneficial.

Here are some treatment approaches to consider:

EMDR: Eye Movement Desensitization and Reprocessing

Eye Movement Desensitization and Reprocessing (EMDR) is a highly effective treatment that began as a modality that used bilateral stimulation of the brain to target trauma symptoms due to PTSD. A plethora of research has established that this bilateral stimulation can actually move traumatic material—along with its associated emotions, images, and body sensations—from being stuck in the more emotional right brain into the more rational left brain. The right brain is where the limbic system and the hippocampus, the emotional and memory centers of the brain, respectively, are predominant. The left brain contains the processing centers that allow us to reprocess and understand our experiences more rationally and effectively from a healthier, more adaptive perspective.

This treatment method has been validated repeatedly over the years, and the preponderance of research has established it as a gold standard for the rapid resolution of trauma. As an EMDR clinician, consultant, and trainer over the past 30 years, I have found that it has literally transformed my practice. My ability to treat trauma has dramatically improved because of having this skill in my clinical toolbox.

Therefore, if you have been a victim of trauma that has affected your ability to stay focused or to regulate your emotions, especially in a way that affects your ability to be mindful while praying, please consider finding an EMDR clinician in your area. You may also be able to find an expert who has experience doing EMDR remotely, which is definitely an option. An EMDR therapist can help you clear the trauma and free yourself from the impediments that affect you.

Over the years, I have often found that people who are stuck in their traumas have difficulty connecting spiritually because their experiences have left them stuck in the past. This makes it difficult for them to be in the present and to truly connect, either spiritually or emotionally. Either the pain is too overwhelming, or they are too shut down from their emotional overload and too disconnected from their emotions to connect with anything else. In either case, EMDR can free you from the baggage you are carrying and allow for a more robust emotional, mindful, and spiritual experience when you pray.

In addition to treating trauma, EMDR can also have a positive effect on the anxiety and ruminations associated with OCD. I use a device called a Theratapper that allows for lengthier, more passive bilateral stimulation. This actually can balance the brain in a way that calms the nervous system and relaxes the intensity of anxiety and overthinking.

This strategy uses a conceptual framework that envisions OCD as a lateralized brain—meaning that it is out of balance—so that the person is either too much in his or her left brain, and thus overthinking and obsessing, or too much in the right brain, and thus too emotional and reactive. The bilateral stimulation produced by this device calibrates the brain and allows it to be more balanced. As a result, thinking is controlled and limited through processing, and the emotions are calmed, contained, and under control. I have quite a few patients who use the Theratapper before prayer because it centers the mind, calms the emotions, and allows for a more mindful prayer experience.

If you find the Theratapper uncomfortable, or if it is difficult to obtain, bilateral tapping of the thighs, or the butterfly hug, which involves crossing one's hands and tapping the upper arms or shoulders, can be quite effective. Some find it preferable because of the need to be able to control the intensity and pacing of the tapping.

The Theratapper can also calm the mind of those who are distracted because of ADHD. This gives them a greater ability to focus and concentrate on their prayers without constant external distractions. Because bilateral stimulation calms the nervous system, it slows down the sometimes frenetic internal world of a person with ADHD. This enables a calmer and more effective ability to pray.

People with ADHD have found that utilizing this inexpensive, easy-to-use device has helped them in many facets of their lives, improving their ability to concentrate and focus, as well as slowing their impulsivity. If you have been diagnosed with ADHD, you definitely want to try this to see how it can have a positive effect on your life, and especially on your ability to pray with greater mindfulness.

IFS: Internal Family Systems Therapy

Internal Family Systems is a wonderful approach to therapy that is based on the premise that we are not unidimensional beings. Rather, each of us has different parts of ourselves that work in sync when we are balanced and functional, or that can conflict with each other, leading to imbalance and dysfunction. IFS is based on the premise that just as we have an external family system of different people who can have difficulty functioning together, we also have an internal family inside of us that can be conflicted and cause a great deal of dysfunction, especially when the unhealthy parts take control.

We all have a core Self that represents who we really are, our authentic selves, and how we want to show up in our lives. We also have different parts that have minds, needs, and personalities of their own that often conflict with the goals and values of the Self. People who show up in my office are often being dominated by parts of themselves that are taking them down roads that lead to a lot of pain and dysfunction.

The goal of IFS is to first get in touch with your core Self and to identify what it stands for and what it wants to achieve for you. IFS supports and strengthens the Self in demonstrating greater leadership and taking more control. It helps you identify the various wounded or damaged parts of yourself that are carrying burdens from the past. These burdens may interfere with your ability to achieve your goals. The ultimate goal is for the Self to direct your parts—as opposed to the dysfunctional parts, such as anger and addictive behavior, controlling the Self and causing problems in your life. Self-leadership thus empowers people to live their lives the way they want rather than allowing these various parts to be in control and cause problems that lead to distress and disempowerment.

IFS calls for setting up an internal "family therapy session," which allows for a dialogue between the Self and the parts. In this dialogue, the Self first appreciates what those parts have gone through that led to their existence and their need to be in control (for instance, to protect or defend you). It then challenges those parts to release their hold on you, allowing you to achieve the goals that the core Self has established. I have found that this internal dialogue can be a powerful impetus for change, and it can profoundly impact your ability to achieve the goals that your wounded parts have blocked or thwarted.

In regard to our discussion of mindful prayer, the goal is to get in touch with your core Self, which wants to have a deeper spiritual experience and connect with God in a more meaningful way. Strengthening your connection with your core Self and focusing on all the reasons you wish to be more spiritually connected will enable you to have that internal dialogue. Then you can empower the Self to regain control of the parts that have blocked your ability to connect spiritually.

DBT: Dialectical Behavior Therapy

Dialectical Behavior Therapy (DBT) is a structured, highly effective, skill-based treatment program that focuses on the skills you need in order to lead a stable and effective life across several dimensions. It addresses four areas of functioning: Distress Tolerance, Emotional Regulation, Mindfulness, and Interpersonal Effectiveness, and it allows you to develop concrete skills that can help you improve your abilities in these areas.

It operates within a group format, but a DBT group is not a typical therapy group that involves a lot of emotional and interpersonal processing. Instead, it follows a specific, structured format that covers each area of functioning. This format includes discussions and exercises that focus on developing different skills. I have found that it has had an enormous impact on the patients who participate, some of whom have repeated the cycle of sessions because they found DBT so valuable that they wanted to reinforce what they learned.

DBT's first three areas of functioning are the most relevant to mindful prayer. Learning how to manage stress and tolerate distressing situations can help you become less emotionally reactive and more focused during prayer. This way, whatever negative experiences you are having in your life won't get in the way of being mindful. Similarly, being more emotionally regulated and in control of distracting negative emotions can greatly assist you in focusing effectively during prayer. Mindfulness skills can help you become more present and in the moment, which can be extremely helpful in your goal of praying more mindfully. These particular skills can be most useful not only in achieving mindful prayer, but also in being more mindful in general.

The book that I use to structure the DBT program is *The Dialectical Behavior Therapy Skills Workbook,* written by my favorite psychology author, Dr. Matthew McKay, along with Drs. Jeffrey Wood and Jeffrey Brantley. If you feel that you could benefit from developing these skills for reaching the goal of mindful prayer or self-improvement in general, I encourage you to find and join a local group. Alternatively, you could buy the book and work on it yourself. It can be a valuable asset in your journey to self-actualization and a deeper spiritual experience.

12-Step Programs

As previously discussed, addictions can have a serious, detrimental effect on your spirituality and your ability to focus on prayer. Being preoccupied with the urges and cravings associated with drug and alcohol addictions, or with getting the next emotional high from a sexual encounter, a gambling experience, a shopping spree, or food engorgement, can keep you from connecting with your higher spiritual self.

Most of the addicts I have worked with report that they feel spiritually blocked by their addictions. This makes sense because being connected spiritually and engaging in addictive behaviors that conflict with your religious or spiritual values are mutually exclusive. It's difficult to be spiritually connected and, more specifically, to connect through meaningful prayer, when you are acting out sexually, drowning yourself in alcohol or drugs, or escaping your inner self and your internal pain through other behavioral addictions that cause shame and despair.

If you are struggling with an addiction that is blocking you from having the rich spiritual life that you want, you can also consider a 12-step program. These programs support people who are struggling with addictions and holds them accountable, bringing them together in meetings where they can share their experiences in order to encourage and inspire one another to work toward sobriety.

There are 12-step programs for alcoholism (AA), narcotics (NA), sex addiction (SA or SAA), gambling (GA), compulsive eating (OA), and several others. They involve "working the steps," that is, systematically working through 12 steps that help lead toward sobriety. These programs can be highly effective in helping people gain control over their addictions and lead more stable and productive lives. Living a sober life without being plagued by obsessiveness and compulsive behaviors can take you a long way toward reestablishing a spiritual connection.

Twelve-step programs also have a spiritual foundation, in that they encourage people to connect with their "Higher Power" and to use that spiritual connection to empower them in their journey toward sobriety. These programs frequently use the powerful mantra "Let go and let God" as a prompt, urging participants to let their spiritual connection guide them, instead of giving in to the urge to act out their particular addiction. These programs do not encourage any specific religious belief system. Instead, they encourage a deeper connection with your spirituality and Higher Power to strengthen your resolve to overcome addiction. These programs can obviously help you achieve the goal of mindful prayer by working toward eliminating the addictive behaviors that are blocking your spirituality. They can also help you reconnect, or possibly connect for the first time, with your spiritual core.

Medication

As a clinical psychologist, I was trained to believe in the dictum, "It's about skills, not pills." However, as I developed a deeper understanding of the complexity of the disorders that I was treating and, more importantly, the involvement of physiological factors in the issues my patients were facing, I came to appreciate the role of psychiatry in helping to treat patients whose issues are more grounded in their biology, as opposed to their psychology. I realized that disorders that are more genetic in origin call for a treatment plan using psychiatric medication as the primary mode of treatment, whereas psychotherapy may be more supportive and can assist in compliance and stability issues.

This is particularly the case in neurogenetically based disorders such as Schizophrenia, Bipolar Disorder, and certain types of familial depression that are clearly inherited.

Medication is absolutely essential when dealing with these disorders; treatment would definitely be ineffective without it.

More pertinent to our discussion, however, it is also true that psychotropic medication can be very helpful if you are dealing with less serious issues such as anxiety, overthinking, distractibility, concentration problems, and non-genetic instances of depression. If your goal is to be a calmer, focused, more mindful person who can concentrate when praying without being hindered by these issues, you should definitely consider a trial of medication. At least, it may be worthwhile to consult a psychiatrist who can educate you about the possible positive effects of a potential medication (as well as the possible side effects). That way, you could make an informed, logical decision about whether medication is right for you, rather than relying on emotionally-based resistance that could block you from even considering pharmacological treatment that could really help you.

A comprehensive review of all the types of available medications is beyond the scope of this section. However, I can provide an overview of possible options that a psychiatrist could prescribe to help someone be calmer and more focused.

Generally speaking, we will review three broad categories of medications that are most often considered when dealing with the issues we have discussed.

The first are Selective Serotonin Reuptake Inhibitors (SSRIs), which include well-known medications such as Prozac, Zoloft, Celexa, and Paxil. They allow for a gradual increase in serotonin—an important neurotransmitter that is essential for optimal brain functioning. Another SSRI, Luvox, is especially effective with symptoms associated with OCD, so consider it if that is your diagnosis, and if obsessive thinking is interfering with your ability to pray mindfully.

Although SSRIs are generally considered to be antidepressants, the increase in serotonin can also help alleviate symptoms of anxiety, OCD, and emotional dysregulation, all of which can impede the ability to pray intently. These medications are non-addictive and non-sedating. Over time, they can be quite effective in helping you manage your emotions and be calmer in general.

Other medications that are not SSRIs but can also be helpful in alleviating anxiety include Buspar and Wellbutrin. Anti-anxiety medications, also called anxiolytics, such as Xanax, Ativan, and Valium, can be used for more immediate and temporary relief of more severe anxiety, but can also be addictive and sedating. Therefore, use caution when considering this class of medication, which generally is not recommended except for severe, acute cases of anxiety. Stimulant medications such as Ritalin, Adderall, Vyvanse, Concerta, and Focalin can be effective in reducing the effects of ADHD, and can help you become less distracted and more able to focus when trying to pray.

Mood stabilizers such as Lithium, Depakote, and Lamictal are necessary for Bipolar Disorder and other disorders, such as Borderline Personality Disorder, which are characterized by instability of mood, emotions, and behavior. Finally, if you have been diagnosed with any type of psychotic disorder or severe OCD, anti-psychotic medications can be helpful, if not necessary, to clear your mind of all the noise and voices inside you and to help you achieve any level of normal functioning. There are generally two classes of these types of medications: the traditional, typical anti-psychotics used for more serious psychotic disorders such as schizophrenia, and what are called atypical anti-psychotics, such as Abilify, Geodon, and Risperdal, for more severe cases of OCD that involve disordered thinking, which may cause a person's worries to be more distorted and out of reality.

This discussion is merely an attempt to give a cursory overview of the options available for those whose challenges in focusing or being emotionally in control are sufficient for them to consider medication as a possible solution to deal with the symptoms that are interfering with their ability to be mindful during prayer. It is not meant to provide medical advice or to recommend a particular medication. The purpose is simply to educate and inform. If you feel that your challenges have advanced to such a degree of severity that you should consider medication, please consult a psychiatrist who can help you decide what medication is right for you.

Therapeutic psychedelics

As I discussed earlier, in recent years I have become involved in psychedelic-supported psychotherapy after reviewing the studies that yielded such positive results with treatment-resistant trauma, addiction, and depression. What I experienced with that first patient amazed me. The protocol has three parts, beginning with a meeting about intentions, where the individual states what he or she hopes to achieve by undertaking the journey. Then comes the actual psychedelic experience, followed by a session on integration to bring together the intentions and the patient's actual experience. The entire process was intense and had a meaningful impact on both the patient and me. The patient uncovered deep, early wounds and was able to communicate the intense feelings about his mother which fueled his need to anesthetize his emotional pain through addiction. It was truly a transformative experience, and the integration session that put everything together for him enabled him to get his addiction under control within a few short months after years of trying unsuccessfully.

Since that first intervention, I have participated in more than a dozen such journeys, and I continue to be impressed with the results. More pertinent to our discussion, psilocybin seems to have a particular ability to inspire intense spiritual experiences that can truly catalyze a deeper spiritual awareness. I experienced a particularly dramatic example with a German patient who grew up completely secular, and who actually considered himself to be an avowed atheist. At the peak of his experience with psilocybin mushrooms, he became very emotional and called out that he felt the presence of God; he also saw what he thought were angels and actually felt them touching him warmly. He had never experienced anything even remotely spiritual in his life, and this was truly a radical change for him. After the intervention, he explored other ways to develop his spirituality, and has literally become a different, more humble, spiritually connected person as a result.

For those of you who feel spiritually blocked or alienated, this type of intervention could be a good option if you are troubled enough, brave enough (and adventurous enough) to give it a try. But first, do the research yourself, consider what I discovered about these medicines, and then decide for yourself if this is something for you to explore further. Several people who have gone through this journey with me reported that their general feeling of connectedness with God, as well as their ability to be more mindful and intentional during prayer, was greatly enhanced as a result. If this is your goal, then it may be advisable to find a facilitator you can relate to in terms of religious practice, who shares your religious affiliation, and who "speaks your language" with regard to spiritual connection.

Alternative Treatments

As someone who has been steeped in the world of alternative medicine for decades, I often recommend natural approaches to medicine and suggest that people generally explore various options in terms of alternative treatments. Natural remedies for anxiety can be highly effective in reducing the intensity of these feelings, which can interfere with the ability to pray mindfully, or even to pray at all.

Supplements that contain valerian root, kava, lavender, chamomile, and elderflower are all excellent choices to help with anxiety and tension, and to calm the nervous system. Herbs such as St. John's Wort have been found to be helpful with certain types of depression, as have amino acids, such as 5-HTP, which can build up levels of serotonin in the brain. Other amino acids, such as l-theanine and l-tryptophan, are natural relaxants and can also help induce sleep. Taking these remedies can help you become a much calmer person and greatly enhance your ability to enter the world of prayer while feeling tranquil and centered.

Studies have also found that acupuncture can have a significant impact on calming the nervous system, facilitating greater concentration and focus. Although I primarily use it personally for pain management and muscle relaxation, acupuncture treatment has a profound effect on my level of tension and stress. It takes me to a "zone" that helps me feel more connected, both emotionally and spiritually.

Another method, cranial-sacral therapy, involves deliberate manipulation of the cranial and sacral areas of the spine. It can have an effect on the nervous system by releasing pent-up energy that could be holding you back from having a spiritual experience.

Yoga is widely regarded as a first-line treatment for trauma, given the physical and mental effects it has on trauma victims. Again, although I use yoga to work on my chronic back issues, I have also found that it takes me to a place of calmness and centeredness, which also helps with prayer. In fact, many spiritual leaders use yoga as a prelude to prayer services to help their congregants prepare for prayer and access their spiritual energy.

Physical Exercise

Exercise can have a profound effect on well-being in general, and on the ability to be more calm and relaxed. Clinical research has shown that even as few as 20 minutes of vigorous exercise can produce hormones such as endorphins and enkephalins that produce an experience called "runner's high." The root of the word "endorphin" is similar to that of "morphine," and the two are also chemically related. Exercise that releases endorphins can cause feelings of mild euphoria, something that some people have likened to an exuberant spiritual experience. It can also produce a profound sense of well-being that, if followed by prayer, can deeply enhance the spiritual experience. Quite a few people I know run or swim or ride a bicycle first thing in the morning before they go to prayer services, because they feel that it helps them prepare for prayer by energizing their spirits and cleansing their minds.

If you do have an exercise regimen, or if you choose to adopt one, it would be helpful to establish the intention of using it as a means of opening your emotional and cognitive channels to prepare for prayer. As we have discussed previously, having an intention to accomplish something makes it more likely to happen. So, before you begin to exercise in the morning, think about how you want to deepen your prayer experience. This is also another way of accomplishing mindfulness; intentionality enhances your ability to be more mindful by sharpening your focus on what you wish to experience.

Nature

Since we are talking about being outside to exercise, we should also mention that just being outdoors surrounded by nature can enhance your prayer experience. By appreciating the beauty of what God has created—the trees, the birds, flowers, the blue sky, even the cloud formations—you can feel more spiritually connected and allow yourself to deepen your prayers. For this reason, many prayer groups and retreats are specifically held outdoors. Being in nature seems to enhance the spirituality of prayer.

However, it should be noted that being outdoors actually may be challenging if you are easily distracted by external stimuli, as in the case of ADHD. This can make it harder for you to be mindful and to concentrate on what you are trying to pray for or to focus on your specific prayers. If you are easily distracted, being in an environment with limited distractions may be more suitable for you, so this may be something to consider.

However, in the case of OCD, where people are more distracted by internal stimuli that plague their minds, being outside and noticing all the wonderful things around them can actually help them be more mindful and focused. Being in nature can take you out of your head and allow you to connect to God through appreciating all that He has created.

Music

Listening to music can stir your soul. Music from your past or songs with a particular message that touches you can open you to a richer prayer experience. Some types of music have a unique quality that can evoke emotions and affect your ability to pray in a more spiritually connected way. It could be music that is spiritual in nature, beautifully orchestrated classical music, or simply a ballad that stirs your emotions for whatever reason.

Music has been an important part of my life ever since I learned how to play the piano and guitar as a child. In time, I also learned how to achieve a deeper spiritual experience through playing and singing songs of a spiritual nature. My father, who was a cantor at our synagogue in the small town in Virginia where I grew up, played records all the time in our living room. Our Sabbath meals were filled with song, and the memories of those meals still affect me deeply today.

You, too, probably have your own connection with music in a unique and special way. Tapping into the music that touches you and brings out your emotions can help you transition into prayer by setting the context of connecting with God. Develop an inventory of songs or music that bring out your emotions or spirituality, and develop a playlist that can help you get into the mood for connecting and praying. Music can significantly enhance the experience.

The psychedelic facilitator with whom I work on interventions actually asks the participants to prepare a playlist of music that moves them. Some focus on classical music, some hard rock, some spiritual music, whereas others choose songs from their earlier lives when they were younger and life was simpler. They have headphones on and listen to these songs as the medicine takes effect, which dramatically affects the intensity of the experience. Sometimes, the facilitator played the music out loud so we could join in the experience. I must admit that there were times when I was deeply affected and moved to tears by the music being played, and I wasn't even doing the trip!

So, if music is part of your life, and you want to beautify your experience with prayer in a way that enhances your ability to pray more mindfully with a deeper emotional connection, try to develop your own playlist of songs that move you, and play some of them before you pray. You will see what a difference it can make to free yourself from distractions and to allow yourself to connect with your heart instead of getting stuck in your head.

Spiritual Counseling

Over the years of my clinical practice, I have often found it enormously helpful to have a team of spiritual advisors and clergy members who can help patients struggling with their spiritual connection or those who may have "left the fold." To wit, I have in my contacts several rabbis, ministers, a priest, and even an imam who I have found particularly sensitive and effective in working with souls who need mending. These clergy people have the ability to become a safe place for spiritual healing and inspiration, or to provide a spiritual "welcome back" for those who have become alienated from their spiritual roots. They can also be helpful resources for those who have not gone off the path, but who are looking for more spiritual inspiration or for someone to study with or learn from who can enhance their spiritual connection.

I highly recommend finding someone within your religious community with whom you can develop a relationship. That person can help you feel more connected and can work more specifically on ways to improve your ability to pray with more intention and purpose. Allow your spiritual guide to inspire you to pray in ways you haven't been able to do previously, both regarding the mechanics of prayer, but also within the broader context of a richer spiritual life.

In the venerable Jewish anthology *Ethics of Our Fathers*, which represents a plethora of moral and ethical principles and guidelines in the Jewish religion, one axiom that stands out in this regard says, "Make for yourself a Rabbi." This can be more loosely translated as "get yourself a spiritual advisor." However, it is noteworthy that the Hebrew word used translates as "make," not "find" or "get." The commentaries note that the word "make" is used deliberately because it signifies the need to be more active in not just obtaining a spiritual advisor, but also in continually "making" or developing that relationship on an ongoing basis, a relationship that can last a lifetime. This relationship with a spiritual advisor can nurture, inspire, and maintain your spiritual life for many years.

Language

Here's one final note that I hope will be helpful in enhancing your prayer experience. For those of you whose religious prayer rituals are in a foreign language, such as Hebrew, Latin, or Arabic, it may be difficult to be mindful when you are struggling to understand the meaning of the prayers that you are reading. Certainly, if you have no idea what you are praying about, having a meaningful spiritual experience will be a struggle.

The first suggestion is to take the time to go over the English translation of your prayers, or a translation in your native language, and to have a general idea of what you are saying and praying about. This will undoubtedly contribute to a more meaningful, mindful prayer experience, since you will at least have a general idea of what you are focusing on for each prayer.

Second, if you intend to commit to a lifetime of serious prayer in your particular religion, and its prayers are in a foreign language, you may want to invest in a serious language course. Then you can at least read in the language of your prayers and eventually understand enough to become fully engaged in the prayers in a way that will be immensely more meaningful.

Finally, in the short run, or perhaps in the long run, you may find it more expedient and realistic to just get a prayer book that is translated into your native language, and pray in that language, rather than trying to understand the prayers in the original tongue. Some find it difficult to learn a new language, and others find the struggle to understand the prayers to be an impediment to being mindful while praying. Praying in your native tongue can greatly enhance your prayer experience, making it far more meaningful and giving it a more profound impact.

So, now that we have completed our discussion of solutions to overcoming spiritual impediments, let's shift toward the importance of maintaining a spiritual connection.

CHAPTER 7

Maintenance

Whenever you embark on a journey of change toward any type of self-improvement, the goal is not only to accomplish the desired change, but also to maintain the gains you have achieved. Otherwise, your efforts to establish real, sustained change will be futile. So, let's explore some ways you can sustain your efforts over time, so you can greatly enhance your ability to be mindful when praying throughout your life.

Definitions

The definition of the word "maintenance" depends on how it is used. Within the context of our discussion of mindful prayer, or of any change you are committed to, maintenance can mean the ongoing continuation of something you have undertaken (definition is mine). It can also refer to a sustained effort to focus on the intended behavioral, cognitive, or emotional goals that you have established for yourself. So, regarding mindful prayer, maintenance really means that you want to "keep your eye on the ball," and keep up whatever you have achieved regarding your prayer experience. If you achieved a deeper level of prayer, or you feel that you are more mindful and focused, you want to maintain that over time and not allow it to wane as time passes.

Let's examine the different elements to consider when discussing maintenance.

Commitment

Being committed to something means you have taken on the responsibility of achieving a particular goal, and you intend to keep that pledge in the long run. Commitment requires the maturity to recognize the importance of the changes you have achieved and to put a plan in place to maintain them indefinitely. It also means that you will make a conscious effort not to allow any distractions or changes in your situation to keep you from continuing on your journey.

For the purpose of our discussion, this means you are completely committed to the goal of praying mindfully, and you fully intend to make it a lifelong endeavor. Your intention is that this will become your new baseline or norm, and from now on, your experience with prayer will be more focused, intentional, and mindful.

Stability

Maintenance requires a certain degree of stability, which means that who you are and what you do are the same today as yesterday and will be the same tomorrow. Stable people have a high degree of consistency in their lives. They are dependable and can be counted on to fulfill their commitments.

People who are stable are impervious to the influences around them and have the ability to resolve inner conflicts that could keep them from being consistent. Regardless of what is happening in their lives, they continue to be who they want to be and to do what they intend to do. They do not allow anything to get in the way of their commitments or responsibilities.

It's important for you to attain a level of emotional and cognitive stability so you can maintain the gains that you achieve in becoming more mindful when praying. Working on being a more stable person will pay many dividends in general and will help you have a more stable, consistent practice of mindful prayer.

Structure

Maintaining any behavior requires structure because it increases the likelihood that your achievements will be consistent over time. For example, having a regular prayer schedule supports consistency and develops an expectation that there is a time to set aside all distractions and prepare for prayer, thus hopefully increasing the probability that your experience with prayer will be more mindful.

People who structure their schedules tend to be more stable and deliberate in the way they live their lives. They tend to be less distractible and more focused. If you self-reflect and realize that your life is not as structured as you would like, adopt the positive goal of finding ways to incorporate a schedule into your routine. Start with a weekly schedule and then work on a daily one that will allow you to feel a sense of order in your life. The feeling that your life is more in order also gives you a greater ability to be focused and mindful while praying because it greatly diminishes any concerns or worries about things being out of control.

Having a sense of order in your life can contribute considerably to a greater sense of stability. Generally, people who are structured tend to be more stable. As we discussed, this can contribute to a greater ability to be more mindful in general, and it can enhance the ability to engage in mindful prayer.

Self-reinforcement

There is a basic behavioral principle that a reinforced behavior is more likely to recur. That is, any effort or incremental change that people notice and reward has a greater chance of being repeated than a behavior that goes unnoticed or ignored. Taking the time to acknowledge yourself for accomplishing any of the goals we have discussed will greatly enhance the probability that you will maintain these changes over time.

Self-affirmations can be very helpful in this regard. Having a repository of positive mantras or things that you say to yourself that are complimentary or encouraging can build self-esteem and lead to a greater likelihood that your efforts to change will continue to improve your experience in prayer. Phrases such as "Good job!", "Great effort!" or "Look how much better you are doing!", as trite as they may seem, can actually reinforce your efforts to improve your ability to pray more effectively.

One final word about self-reinforcement: engaging in a mindful experience of prayer isn't always easily done. As we have discussed, it takes a lot of focus, concentration, discipline, and mindful effort. Having a positive, "can-do" attitude toward your general ability to accomplish challenging goals, along with a healthy dose of self-confidence, can go a long way in achieving your long-term goal of maintaining a practice of mindful prayer. Therefore, having the intention and making an ongoing effort to notice and compliment yourself for your efforts and actual progress, will help maintain that progress over time.

Relapse Prevention

You may think the topic of relapse prevention is a bit strange to include in a discussion about mindful prayer. It's true that this concept is better suited to the subject of addiction. Yet, there is a parallel here that can be helpful when discussing long-term maintenance of a newly changed behavior.

I define a relapse as a regression to a previous maladaptive pattern of behavior, after a period of improvement or sobriety. Within the context of our discussion about mindful prayer, we are trying to move away from patterns of distraction, inattentiveness, obsessive thinking, and negativity. Once you have worked on achieving the goals of being less distracted, obsessive, and negative, along with being more attentive and mindful, it's important to continue to work on not reverting back to old patterns that made it difficult for you to be mindful during prayer in the first place. A plan for preventing this regression (or relapse) should include concrete steps to ensure that you won't revert to old patterns of maladaptive behaviors. It is similar to the relapse prevention plans I give patients who are recovering from addictions.

Once you have achieved a sufficient, fulfilling level of mindfulness in your prayer practice, you may want to develop a plan of action you can implement to prevent a regression back to previous pattern of mindless, distracted prayer. Consider these suggestions:

➤ A practice of daily meditation

➤ Daily intentions to be mindful, in general and/or specifically regarding prayer

➤ Having a prayer partner you check in with every morning, so that you can prompt each other to be mindful and focused during prayer

➤ Deep breathing before prayer to clear your mind of distractions

➤ Maintaining a daily prayer journal, describing how mindful you were during prayer and what you felt you accomplished

➤ Keeping track on a daily basis of how connected you feel to your experience of prayer

➤ Keeping track daily of how connected you feel to God

➤ Every day, reinforce your efforts and progress toward praying mindfully

➤ Frequently remind yourself how frustrating it was to be unfocused and distracted during prayer and how strongly you want to avoid going back there

➤ Reach out for help to your prayer partner or a member of the clergy to whom you feel close if you sense that your ability to be mindful during prayer is beginning to slip, and you need a "booster shot" of spiritual connection

CONCLUSION

The Rewards of Achieving
a Deeper Connection

Living a spiritually enriched life, especially through an ongoing meaningful experience of prayer, has been associated with a wide array of physical, mental, and emotional benefits. An overview of randomized controlled studies by the US National Institutes of Health regarding the physical benefits of regular prayer and meditation showed that people who prayed or meditated improved consistently in a wide range of physiological measures, including:

➤ Reduced ambulatory blood pressure

➤ Slowed heart rate

➤ Increased levels of serotonin and melatonin

➤ Reduction in sleep disturbances

➤ Improved immune functioning

➤ Reduced levels of stress hormones

➤ Reduced perception of pain

Other studies have shown that the positive emotional effects of prayer and meditation include:

➤ Reduced levels of depression

➤ Increased positive mood states

➤ Reduced levels of anxiety

➤ Decreased levels of emotional stress

➤ Enhanced self-esteem

➤ Increased improvements in recovery from mental illness

➤ Increases in measures of quality of life in late-stage disease

Prayer also appears to significantly improve cognitive functioning. Numerous studies have shown positive results in people who have a regular practice of praying versus similar people who do not pray. The positive results appeared in the following areas of functioning:

➤ Focus and attention

➤ Reduced distractibility

➤ Improvements in working memory

➤ Enhanced long-term memory retention

➤ Improved mental clarity

➤ Enhanced performance in cognitive tasks

➤ Mitigation against age-related mental decline

Interestingly, prayer and spiritual meditation yielded significantly more robust positive results than secular meditation and relaxation exercises. These results included decreased anxiety and increased positive mood, spiritual health, and pain tolerance. It seems that the spiritual aspect of the meditative process involved in prayer is the salient factor that contributes to all these improvements.

Studies have also shown that people who pray regularly tend to have a higher degree of life satisfaction than those who don't. The theory behind these findings is that people who generally live more meaningful lives tend to be happier and more satisfied. People with a strong spiritual foundation who pray are more likely to find greater meaning in their daily lives. Therefore, it makes sense that they would also be more satisfied with their lives in general.

Working at being more effective in your ability to pray more mindfully can have a positive effect on your general well-being simply because you were able to accomplish an important goal. This achievement can greatly enhance your self-perception as a competent, accomplished person who is able to take on an important goal and get it done. This sense of being competent in achieving your goals cannot be underestimated in terms of personal development, as well as the obvious enhancement in spiritual growth.

Finally, many people find that improving their ability to pray more effectively in terms of focus and mindfulness can lead to the ability to be a more spiritual person in general. For those of you who have found yourself "stuck" spiritually, achieving the goal of having a more meaningful prayer experience can catapult your level of spirituality and connection with God in very significant ways.

A Final Note

It is my fervent prayer that this book will help you in your journey to reach greater spiritual heights and connection. Prayer can be either a frustrating exercise in futility or a deeply meaningful and spiritually enriching experience. I know personally that writing this book, and working hard to actually "practice what I preach," has been invaluable in improving my own prayer experience, which admittedly was a bit of a struggle. I hope you will find that what you have read here is invaluable in developing your spiritual connection in ways you never thought possible.

Acknowledgments

My most valuable teachers have always been my patients. I have learned so much from their many insights and challenges. Over the years, they have inspired me with their grit and determination to become their authentic selves, who they would have been had they not been derailed by circumstances that were beyond their control. They have a truly remarkable ability to transform themselves through therapy, even though it is often arduous work. I will always be grateful to them for trusting me to be their agent of change.

I also am thankful for my equally remarkable (and interminably patient) editor, Erica Meyer Rauzin, who gently shaped the book toward its final version. Her gifted talent in balancing art and form has greatly contributed to my ability to complete this project.

Thanks also to Gary Rosenberg of The Book Couple for another superb publishing job. And thanks to Karen Zarkower, my tireless administrative assistant, for all she does to support all that I do.

I also want to thank my family for their undying support and encouragement.

About the Author

Originally from Newport News, Virginia, Dr. Norman Goldwasser is a clinical psychologist in Miami Beach, Florida. He earned Master's degrees in Clinical Psychology and Industrial-Organizational Psychology, and a Ph.D. in Clinical Psychology summa cum laude from the Virginia Commonwealth University in Richmond.

Trained as a cognitive-behavioral psychologist, his primary focus of treatment and writings has been in the field of trauma. He is widely regarded as an expert in Eye Movement Desensitization and Reprocessing (EMDR), having been a clinician, consultant, and trainer over the past 30 years.

He is an internationally known speaker on various topics including child sexual trauma, marital issues, educational psychology, positive psychology, and spirituality. He has consulted with more than 100 businesses, law and medical practices, hospitals, and educational institutions throughout his career. More recently, he has volunteered in Israel to treat trauma victims, soldiers, and their families and to train therapists to use EMDR.

Dr. Goldwasser's first book, *Breaking the Mirror: Overcoming Narcissism—How to Conquer Self-Centeredness and Achieve Successful Relationships,* has received much critical acclaim. He recently published a second book, *CQ: The Changeability Quotient.*

Dr. Goldwasser is most proud of his seven children, 28 wonderful grandchildren, and three amazing great-grandchildren.

www.ingramcontent.com/pod-product-compliance
Lightning Source LLC
Chambersburg PA
CBHW060637130626
46555CB00002B/844